D0583581

Mies van der Rohe

ALBUQUERQUE ACADEMY
LIBRARY
6400 Wyoming Blvd. N.E.
Albuquerque, N.M. 87109

Mies van der Rohe
The Art of Structure

Werner Blaser

WHITNEY LIBRARY OF DESIGN

an imprint of Watson-Guptill Publications/New York

The German and English texts to this new and expanded edition were originally published in 1985 by Verlag fur Architektur, Zurich, and Frederick A. Praeger, Inc., New York, respectively.

Copyright ©1993 by Birkhäuser Verlag

First published in the United States in 1994 by Whitney Library of Design, an imprint of Watson-Guptill Publications, a division of BPI Communications, Inc., 1515 Broadway, New York, NY 10036.

Library of Congress Cataloging-in-Publication Data

Blaser, Werner, 1924–
   Mies van der Rohe : the art of structure / Werner Blaser.
      p.   cm
   Issued also by Birkhäuser in English and German, 1993
   Includes bibliographical references.
   ISBN 0-8230-3064.4
   1. Mies van der Rohe, Ludwig, 1886–1969—Criticism and interpretation.
2. Architecture—Technological innovations.   3. Architecture, Modern—20th century.
I. Mies van der Rohe. Ludwig, 1886–1969.   II. Title.
NA1088.M65857   1994
720'.92—dc20   93-43337
                                  CIP

All rights reserved. No part of this publication may be reproduced or used in any form or by any means—graphic, electronic, or mechanical, including photocopying, recording, taping, or information storage and retrieval systems—without written permission of the publisher.

Manufactured in Singapore.

First printing, 1994

1 2 3 4 5 6 7 8 9 10 / 03 02 01 00 99 98 97 96 95 94

720.92
BLA
1994

Anyone today in search of new and stimulating ideas in architecture will rediscover the work of the past master Mies van der Rohe. His work, we have reason to believe, still conceals unsuspected treasures of ordering and truth waiting to be unearthed and, even in our day, these can lead to reappraisals and prompt fresh thinking.

This is why it is very important to bring out a new edition of this epochal work by one of the truly great architects of our time. Here, then, in its original form we have the book which Mies authorized in 1964 in Chicago. Only the appendix has been expanded: biography, bibliography and catalogue of works have been supplemented and at the same time the most important books in Mies' library listed.

Finally I have photographed some of Mies' outstanding buildings in their present setting, and it has been brought home to me how relevant they are to our modern world and what a fine example they set. For, after the passage of three decades, they have barely aged at all. And so a hearty "encore" for everyone concerned!

W. B., April 1993

It was about 1910 that I first realized I was embarking on my professional career. At that time the Jugendstil and Art Nouveau movements had run their course. Buildings designed to be worthy representatives of their owners were influenced to a greater or lesser extent by Palladio and Schinkel. But it was the industrial and other purely technical buildings that were the greatest achievements of the period. Those were confused days, and nobody would venture an answer to questions about the nature of architecture. Perhaps it was still too early for an answer. All the same, I posed the question and was determined to find an answer to it.

It was only after the war, in the twenties, that the influence technical developments were beginning to exert on many aspects of life became increasingly apparent. We recognized technology to be a civilizing force and one to be reckoned with. Advancing technology provided the builder with new materials and more efficient methods which were often in glaring contrast to our traditional conception of architecture. I believed, nevertheless, that it would be possible to evolve an architecture with these means.

I felt that it must be possible to harmonize the old and the new in our civilization. Each of my buildings was a statement of this idea and a further step in my search for clarity.

It was my growing conviction that there could be no architecture of our time without the prior acceptance of these new scientific and technical developments. I have never lost this conviction. Today, as for a long time past, I believe that architecture has little or nothing to do with the invention of interesting forms or with personal inclinations.

True architecture is always objective and is the expression of the inner structure of our time, from which it stems.

Contents

Foreword

Mies van der Rohe has evolved his ideas from the basic principles of construction; hence the form of his buildings is the expression of their structure. This book sets out to show how, in his buildings, Mies van der Rohe has made a clearly recognized structure the basis of his construction and thus raised it to the level of an art. This elevation of structure to the level of an art will be illustrated by examples ranging from the simple pattern of a brick wall to the transparent construction of a wall of steel and glass.

Mies van der Rohe has pointed out that the idea that construction must be the basis of the new architecture is not a novel one. It was in fact the point of departure for modern architecture and found expression in Viollet-le-Duc's "Entretiens sur l'Architecture", which appeared at the beginning of the eighteen-sixties. It demands that purposes should be answered honestly and significantly with the means and constructional methods of the time. For Viollet-le-Duc artistic form was not, as for his contemporaries, the question of a new art independent in itself but rather the result of an organized structure. "Toute forme, qui n'est pas ordonnée par la structure, doit être repoussée."

Mies van der Rohe is not interested in inventing new forms; rather, by thinking in terms of construction and technology, his aim is to evolve a clear and simple structure. Amidst the confusion of the "eternally new" in which we live, it is a fulfilment to settle on a consistent form of construction, for, within the scope of a sound and perfected structure, so many variations are possible. He has expressed this idea in these words: "It is absurd to invent arbitrary forms, historical and modernistic forms, which are not determined by construction, the true guardian of the spirit of the times." He believes this concentration on structure can help the architect in his task: "The unswerving determination to dispense with all accessories and to make only what is essential the object of the creative work, the determination to confine oneself to clear structure alone is not a limitation but a great help." Structure in these terms is a constructed system of relations, a constructive form rationally thought out in all its details.

From the very outset Mies van der Rohe's designs were lucid and uncompromising statements of the idea that a clear distinction was to be made between structural and non-structural elements. It is in the Barcelona Pavilion (1929) with its overlapping, non-bearing walls of fine materials, that structure is raised to a perfect work of art. With it a new period of architecture began. Material, structure, space and the restless need for metaphysical security are here made one. The interplay of closed and open spaces is not calculated but realized as part of an inner harmony.

Even the layman can feel the perfect artistry with which Mies van der Rohe handles the surface plane and the structural elements in his buildings, and can appreciate how, by his work and teaching, he enables us to understand those building systems of the past, such as the Doric order, which have created their own structural order. The refinement of the connection between column and roofslab in the "Gallery of the 20th Century" in Berlin (1963) helps us by the very fact of its difference to understand the structures of past epochs.

Mies van der Rohe believes that architecture is not bound to the day nor to eternity but to the epoch. Only a genuine historical movement makes it what it is. Architecture is the interpretation of a happening in history, the genuine consummation of its inner movement, the fulfilment and expression of its essential nature. In his buildings he seeks to express the significant driving forces of our era: the economic order in which we live, the discoveries of science and technology, the fact of the mass society.

In the skeleton-type skyscraper with its glass skin, the curtain wall is raised to the highest level of art and expressed down to the smallest structural detail. The structure in Mies van der Rohe's work determines the entirely flexible arrangement of the plan; and its refinement and classicism are most clearly expressed in the spacious column-free interiors of these one-room buildings where every kind of function can by accommodated.

"Precisely because our building is determined by technology, we may say that only where our purposes find expression in a significant and logical structure are we justified in speaking of architecture. Only where genuine construction meets genuine content can genuine works come into being, and it is genuine works we need, genuine and reflecting their own true nature. We shall give to each thing what belongs to it according to its nature."

Mies van der Rohe's final aim is order and truth, a practical beauty which serves mankind. This spiritual order was defined by Thomas Aquinas as "adaequatio rei et intellectus". It is precisely this truth which is so firmly rooted in the mental character of Mies van der Rohe and in every detail of his work. To grasp this mentally takes time; it presupposes that we are ready to penetrate to the heart of solutions which have been distilled to the ultimate in simplicity. Mies van der Rohe has performed the meritorious service of re-directing architecture along the path to a deeper spiritual plane and thus to an ultimate unity. Through his work we are able to recognize the spiritual nature of architectural problems and find ever new solutions for them in creative freedom.

The approach to structure

It was always a distinguishing feature of Mies van der Rohe's work in Germany that he refused to imitate earlier styles and sought single-mindedly for constructions which articulated the material into a clear and visible structure matched to the purpose of the building and the nature of the material itself. Subjective and merely decorative trimmings were shunned and the law of structure strictly obeyed. He designed many projects which were never executed: they were visionary schemes far in advance of their time. This was absolute architecture pointing the way to the future.

Mies van der Rohe concentrated on the properties of his building material and clearly expressed these in his charcoal drawings and model studies. In his first tower projects, for example, glass was not seen in large surfaces but was broken up by angles for the sake of light reflection and the effect of depth. In the brick villa every wall revealed the character of the brickwork down to the smallest detail. It is astonishing to see that, besides this sensitive treatment of material, flexible interlocking spatial patterns and the free-standing load-bearing wall were already featured in the work of this early period. In the reinforced concrete office building cantilevering was used with convincing skill and a new conception of space created by turning up the floor slabs along their edges. What mattered was invariably the development of structure and constructional possibilities, never arbitrary forms.

Glass skyscraper on a prismatic plan, competition project 1919

The charcoal sketch shows an office skyscraper near the Friedrichstrasse station in Berlin. It is a 20-storey steel skeleton, encased in glass, with one front overlooking the Spree. The triangular shape of the site suggested the prismatic form of the plan. The perspective view clearly shows how the glass surfaces are set at angles so as to fit the outline of the plan and thus produce a rich play of light reflections.

Glass skyscraper on a polygonal plan, project 1920–1921

Studies of light reflections on a glass model led to a polygonal plan being adopted. The curves followed by the glass walls were determined by the lighting needs of the interior, by the appearance of the building mass when seen against the existing buildings in the street, and by the play of reflections it was desired to achieve. The two glass skyscrapers were experiments which matured out of one and the same thought process: to exploit the potentialities of the materials and technology of a new age, and to create something meaningful out of them. For Mies van der Rohe action has always been synonymous with thought: "My ideas guide my hand, and my hand shows whether my idea is any good."

Charcoal drawing: Glass skyscraper on a prismatic plan

Charcoal drawing: Facades of the skyscraper with
non-bearing walls of glass

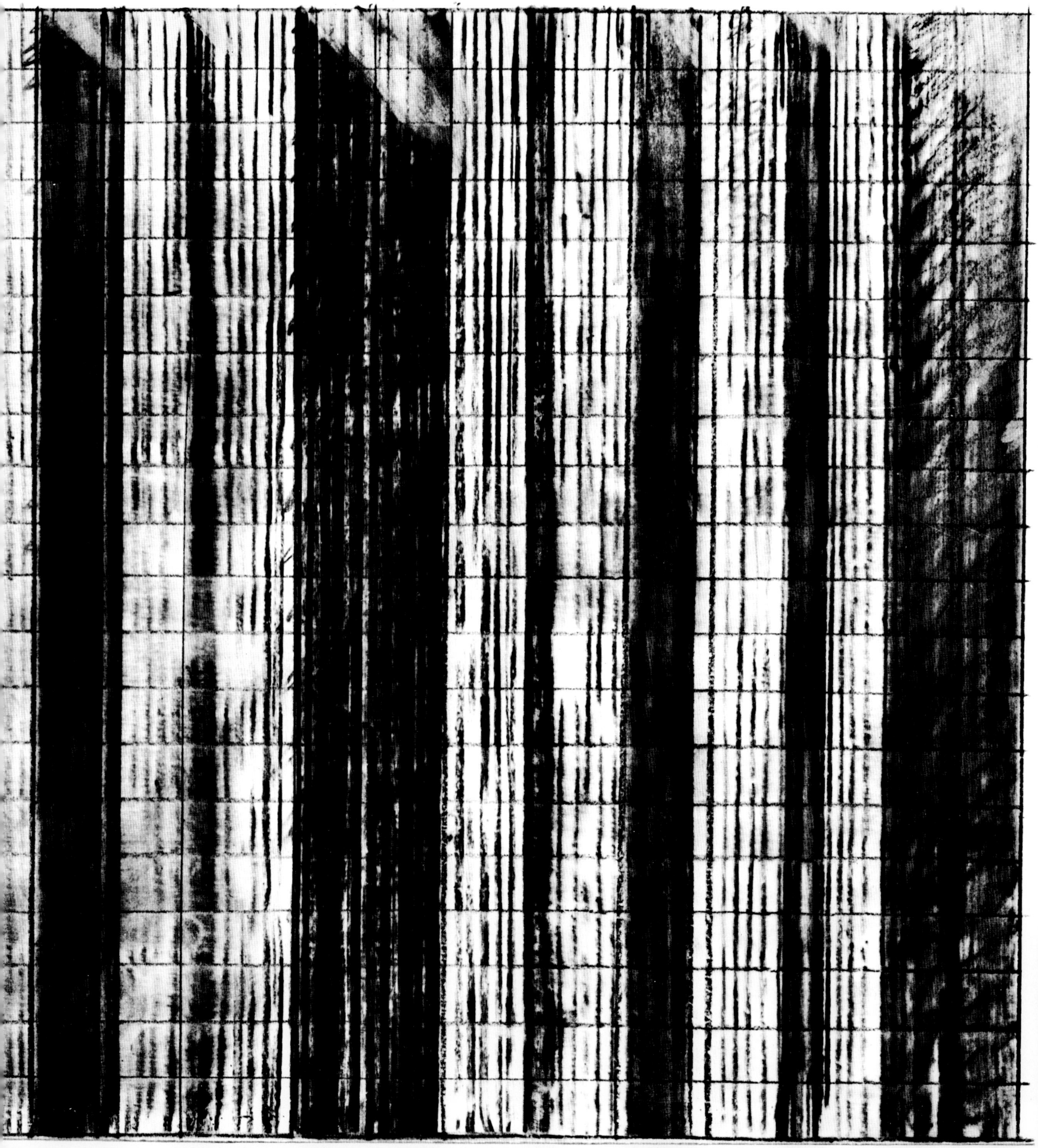

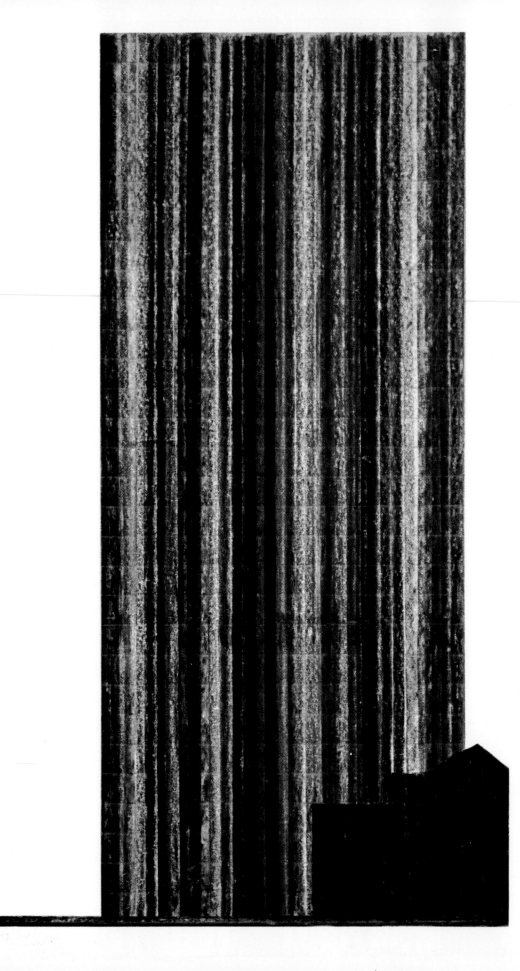

Charcoal drawing: Glass skyscraper on
a polygonal plan

Reinforced concrete building, project 1922

The floors of the office building are formed by cantilevered concrete slabs which are turned up and around at the edges in a U-shape. These niches around the periphery of the building are two metres in height and are used as storage cabinets, thus leaving the interior free and uncluttered. As the ribbon window running round the perimeter is flush with the front of these cabinets, it appears set well back from the facade when viewed from outside. The offices are 16 metres in depth.

The columns of the concrete skeleton are located four metres back from the facade on all sides. Since each floor is one clean space, great flexibility is possible in the layout of offices.

Charcoal drawing: Project for a block of offices in ▷
reinforced concrete with cantilevered floors

ALBUQUERQUE ACADEMY
LIBRARY

Albuquerque Academy
Library
6400 Wyoming Blvd. N.E.
Albuquerque, N.M. 87109

Brick house, project 1923

The garden is divided by three long, straight walls of brick. The villa itself crystallizes round their meeting point. The bearing brick walls are set out as the floor plan requires and connect the interior and exterior. The various living areas in the interior are screened from one another, and yet there is an easy flow of space from one room to the next. There are no corridors.

The flat roof rests on walls in which no openings are cut. Simple means have been used to banish the image of the conventional villa. The plan of the brick villa is a good example of the way in which Mies van der Rohe has developed the art of structure from the very beginning. The structure of a brick wall begins with the smallest unit into which the whole can be divided: the brick. The dimensions are calculated in terms of the basic unit of the brick.

There has been no essential change in the bonding of a brick wall for centuries. Mies' discovery has been to recognize the fundamental law and logic of the material and to unify the walls in a well-proportioned interplay of volumes and open spaces, both inside and outside.

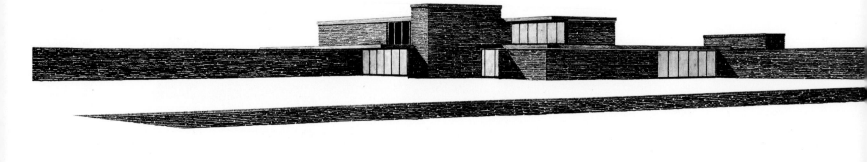

Charcoal drawing: Brick as a material for house
and garden walls

Detail of brick wall   ▷

Villa: Free-standing walls of brick connect indoors   ▷ ▷
and outdoors. Plan, scale 1:200 ($\frac{1}{16}$ ″=1′ − 0 ″)

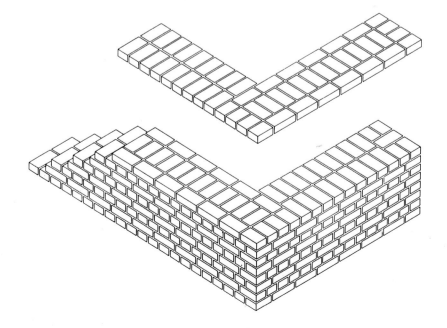

ALBUQUERQUE ACADEMY
LIBRARY

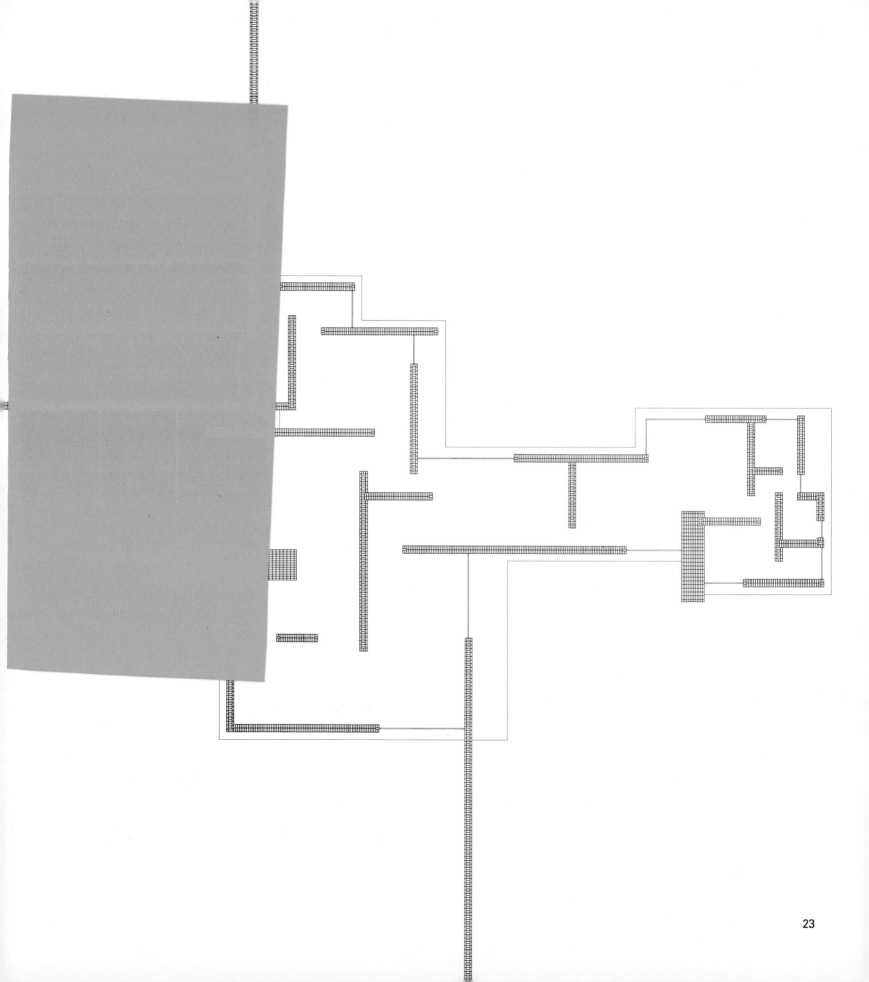

Concrete house, project 1924

The outer-bearing walls of the villa were planned as reinforced concrete slabs. The material allows windows to be cut in the outer wall wherever they are needed. The simple geometrical forms of the facade make the whole look as if it had been cast in a single mould.

The various living areas are independent cubes which are set at angles to each other and form courts or patios. The result is a clearly articulated plan which emphasizes the play of forms between the house, the garden and the natural setting. In the large inner room the roof is supported on columns.

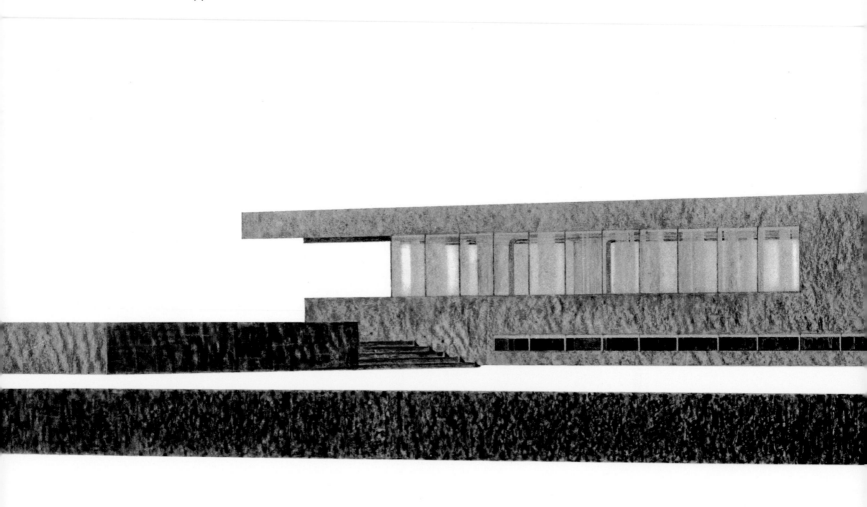

Charcoal drawing: Villa in reinforced concrete.
Cantilevered elements and indentations in the facade

Court houses with steel columns

In court or patio houses the contrast between supporting and supported elements is clearly stated. This design has been largely instrumental in promoting further development towards a flexible plan and the satisfaction of the need for light, air and verdure. The roof is supported on brick walls and an interior system of steel columns. The house and the court are surrounded by brick walls between which are openings; the dimensions of these openings are based on brick modules.

In the German Pavilion at Barcelona Mies van der Rohe first developed non-bearing walls of precious materials arranged with overlapping planes. Here the definition of architecture as "Baukunst" carries special conviction: "Bau" (building) is the static and law-conforming element based on a strict intellectual order, and "Kunst" (art) is the free and creative element which can operate within a clear structure.

German Pavilion at the 1929 World Exhibition in Barcelona

On a site at the World Exhibition in Barcelona there was erected an imposing pedestal measuring 53×17 metres which the visitor had to traverse. Free-standing walls of fine materials enclosed the pavilion and formed a pattern of open and closed spaces. The pavilion had no function to perform other than to look worthy of the country it represented.

The terrace was partly covered by two pools of different sizes and one part was roofed. The roof slab was supported on eight steel columns of cruciform section encased in chromium-plated covers. Honey-coloured golden onyx, green Tinian marble and tinted and frosted glass were the materials of which the overlapping walls were made. An existing block of onyx was split twice, and the slabs, placed one over the other, determined the height of the pavilion (3.10 metres). The only transverse wall to join two others was made of frosted glass and contained lighting which provided diffuse illumination inside and outside the pavilion. The chairs and stools in the interior were of flat chromium-plated steel bars upholstered with cushions of white leather; the tables were topped with slabs of black opal glass. In the water court, one of the roofless demi-patios, stood a figure of a dancer by Georg Kolbe. The terrace was

The interposed walls are independent of the
load-bearing columns

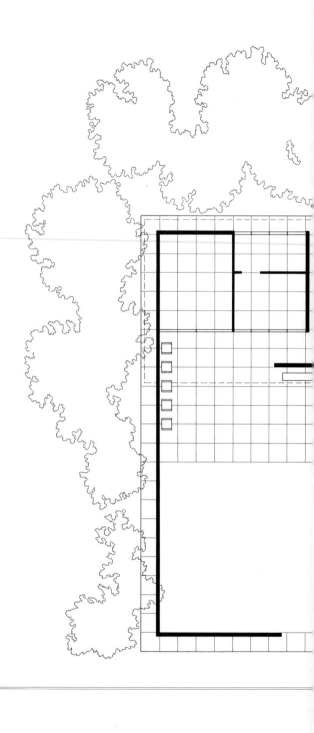

General plan of the Barcelona Pavilion.
Scale 1:200 ($\frac{1}{16}$"=1'−0")

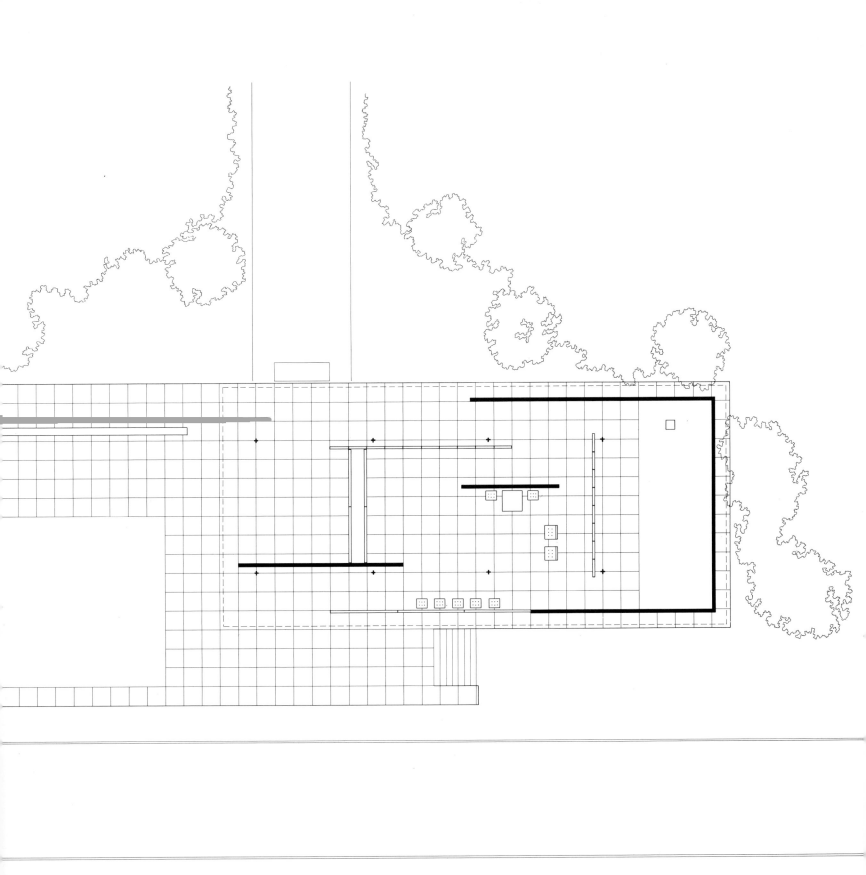

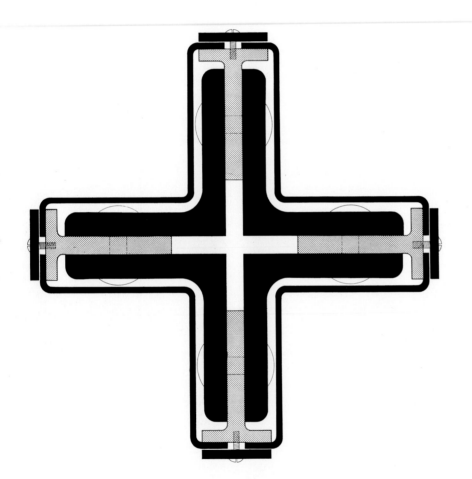

◁ Section of the cruciform columns. Scale 1:5 (2″=1′)

Covered areas. The roof is supported on steel   ▷
columns

Integration of architecture and fine art

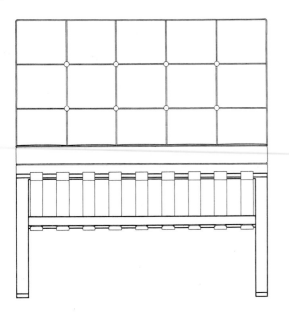

Barcelona chair in steel and leather.
Scale 1:12½ (1"=1'–0")

Integration of architecture and furniture ▷

House in the Alps, project 1934

This sketch was made for the architect's own house in a mountain resort. The interior rooms are defined by walls and large areas of glass. An inner court keeps out the wind and links together inside and outside.

Spanning a valley depression, the house grows out of the land-scape. Mountain and house are one: "The mountain is my house."

Charcoal drawing: House in the Alps

House with three courts, project 1934

This living area for a family is enclosed by a brick wall of full storey height round its perimeter. Part of the area is covered with a roof slab which, supported on slim steel columns, rests upon the brick wall. The system of supports in the interior allows the room to be subdivided as desired. The living rooms can be opened on all sides into the garden, with which they form a pleasing harmony.

How admirably these court houses are suited to living conditions in our big cities! Within an enclosure that excludes all extraneous disturbance, one can live in rooms of choice simplicity, where indoors and outdoors are harmoniously related.

Plan and elevation of the court house.   ▷
Scale 1:200 ($\frac{1}{16}$"=1'-0")

House with three courts, collage with composition   ▷ ▷
by Georges Braque

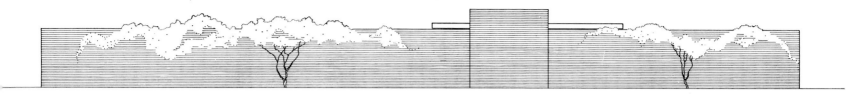

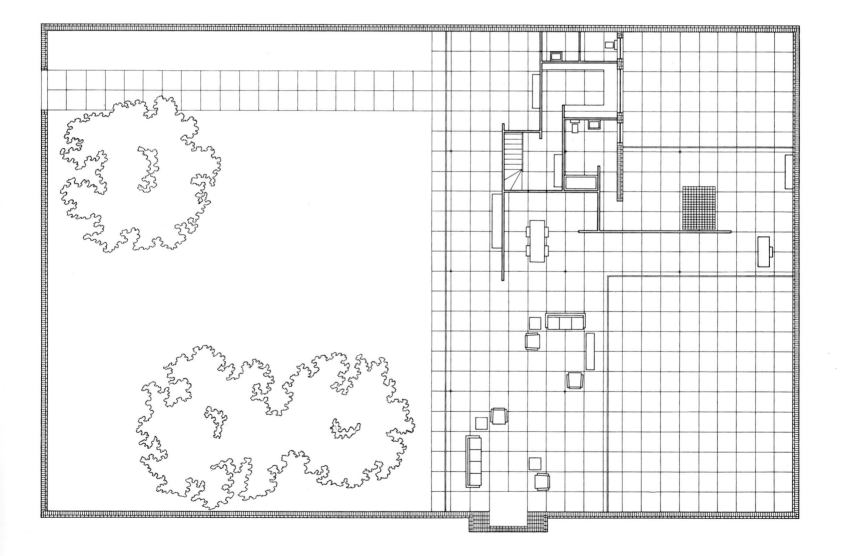

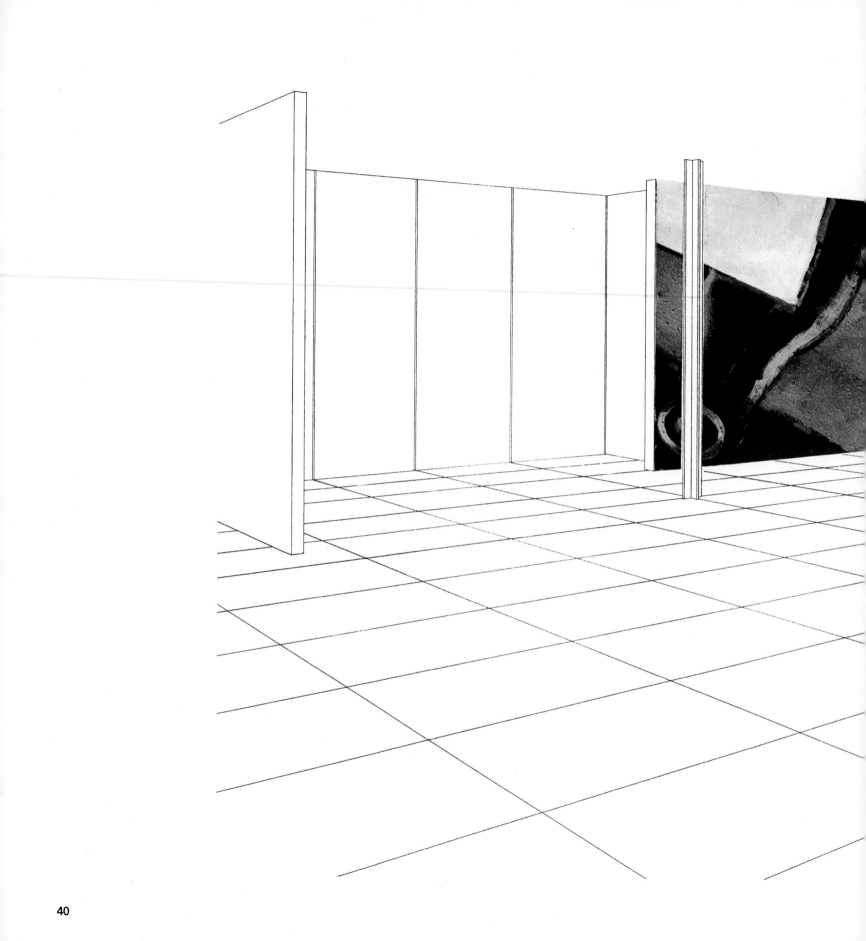

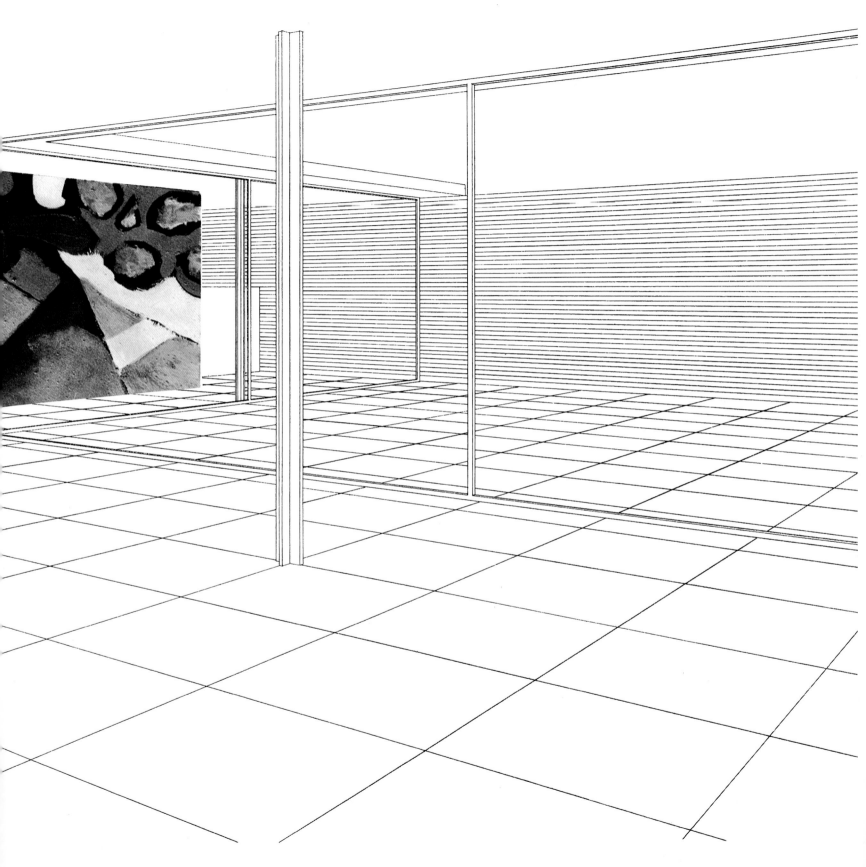

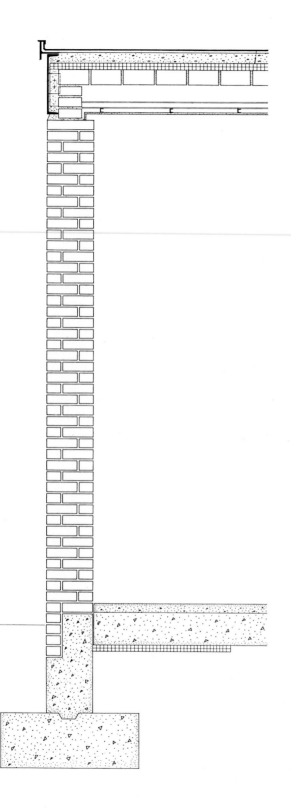

◁ Vertical section of roof and bearing brick wall.
Scale 1:25 (½"=1'–0")

Perspective drawing showing the method of
construction and materials. Term task at the IIT
(Professor Alfred Caldwell's course)

Load-bearing steel columns with glass wall behind.
View into the walled court

44

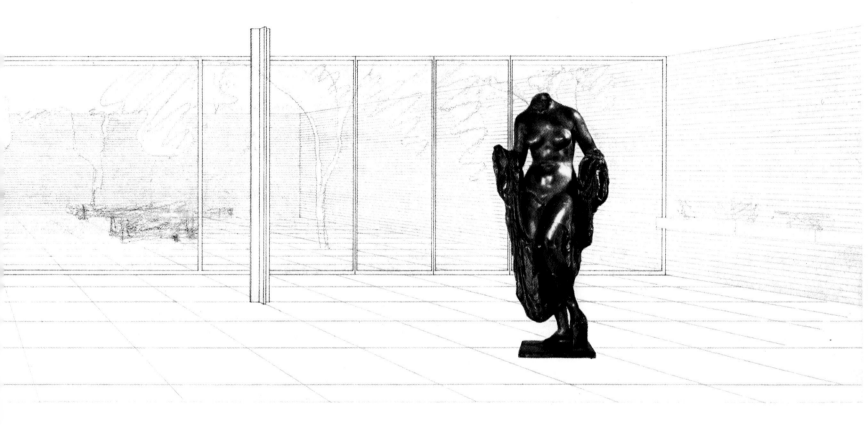

Group of court houses, project 1931

The rectangular site is screened from the outside world by a brick wall round its perimeter. It belongs to a group of three owners whose properties, each of different size, are partitioned off by walls.

All the walls are set on the lines of a planning grid in which the module is a brick. Part of each court is covered by a roof slab under which the rooms flow one into the other. The various living areas open into intimate courts. In these houses all the enclosed space, indoors and outdoors, is used as a living area.

In a town-planning scheme a district of court houses forms a residential zone consisting of circumscribed living areas, each with its own intimate atmosphere. The houses are, as it were, cloisters in which the individual can lead a completely private life.

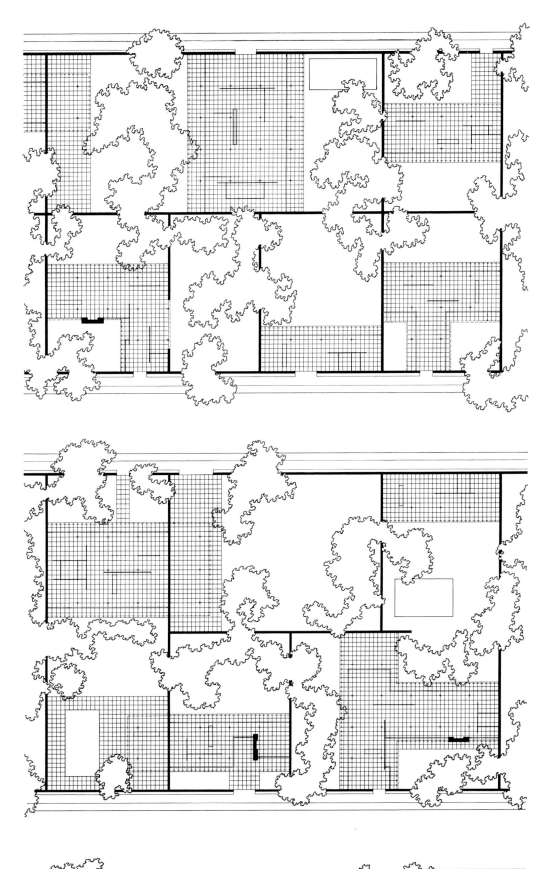

Plan showing part of a development of court
houses with traffic routes. Scale 1:800 (1/64"=1'– 0")

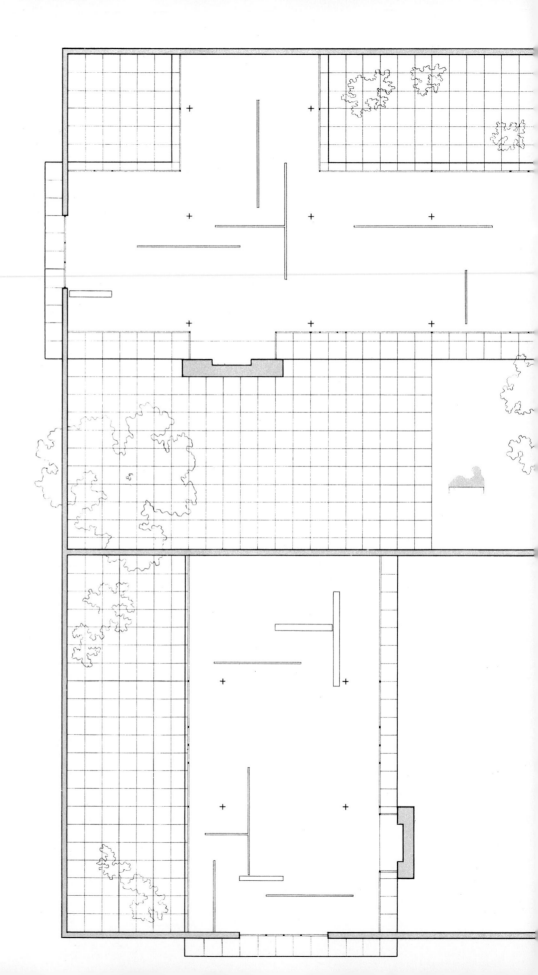

Plan of a group of court houses.
Scale 1:200 (1/16"=1'—0")

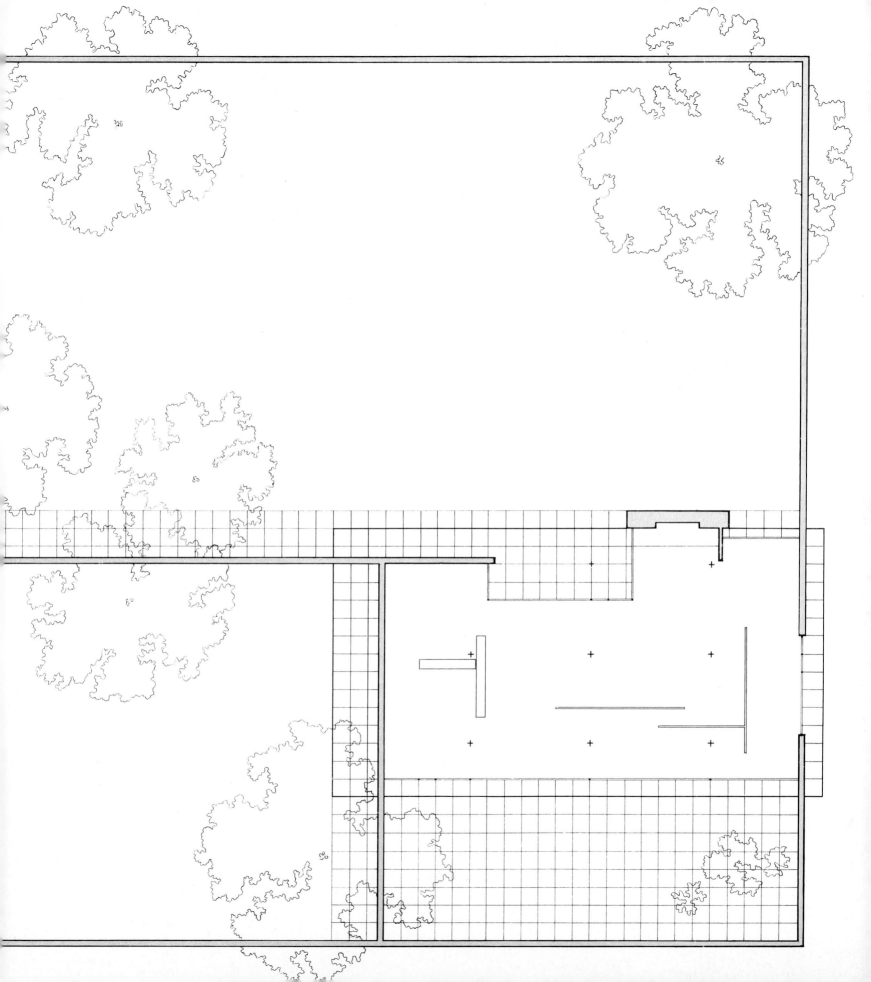

Mies van der Rohe:
Principles of architectural education

The school of architecture has two aims: to train the architect by imparting the necessary knowledge and skills, and to educate him in order that he can make proper use of the knowledge and skills he has acquired. Thus training has practical purposes in view, but education has values. It is the business of education to implant insight and responsibility. It must turn irresponsible opinion into responsible judgment and lead from chance and arbitrariness to the rational lucidity of an intellectual order.

In its simplest forms architecture is rooted in the purely utilitarian but it can reach up through the whole gamut of values into the highest sphere of spiritual existence, into the realm of pure art.

This realization must be the starting point for any system of architectural education. Step by step, it must make clear what is possible, what is necessary and what is significant. This is why the various subjects must be co-ordinated so that there is organic unity at every stage and the student can study all the different aspects of building in their relationships to one another.

Apart from technical instruction, the student should first learn to draw so as to train hand and eye and master his means of expression. Exercises will give him a sense of proportion, structure, form and material, and show him how they are related and what they can express. The student should then get to know the materials and construction of simple buildings in timber, stone and brick, and then go on to find out what can be done with steel and reinforced concrete as building materials. At the same time he should learn how these elements are significantly interrelated and how they are directly expressed in form.

Any material, whether natural or artificial, has its special properties which one must know before one can work with it. New materials and new methods of construction are not necessarily superior. What matters is the way they are handled. The value of a material depends on what we make of it.

After materials and methods of construction, the student must familiarize himself with functions. They must be clearly analysed so that he knows precisely what they involve. It must be clearly understood why and how one building scheme differs from another. What it is that gives it its special character.

Any introduction to the problems of city-planning must teach the fundamentals on which it is based and show clearly how all aspects of building are interconnected and related to the city as an organism.

Finally, and by way of a synthesis of the whole course of instruction, the student is introduced to building as an art. He is taught the essential nature of art, the application of its means and its realization in the building.

But these studies must also include an analysis of the spirit of our times upon which we are dependent. Present and past must be compared for differences and similarities in both a material and spiritual sense. This is why the buildings of the past must be studied and vividly described so as to convey a clear grasp of their essentials. It is not merely a matter of taking their greatness and significance as an architectural criterion but also of realizing that they were bound to a particular non-recurrent historical situation and thus place us under a duty to aspire to our own creative achievements.

Illinois Institute of Technology (IIT): ▷
Original project

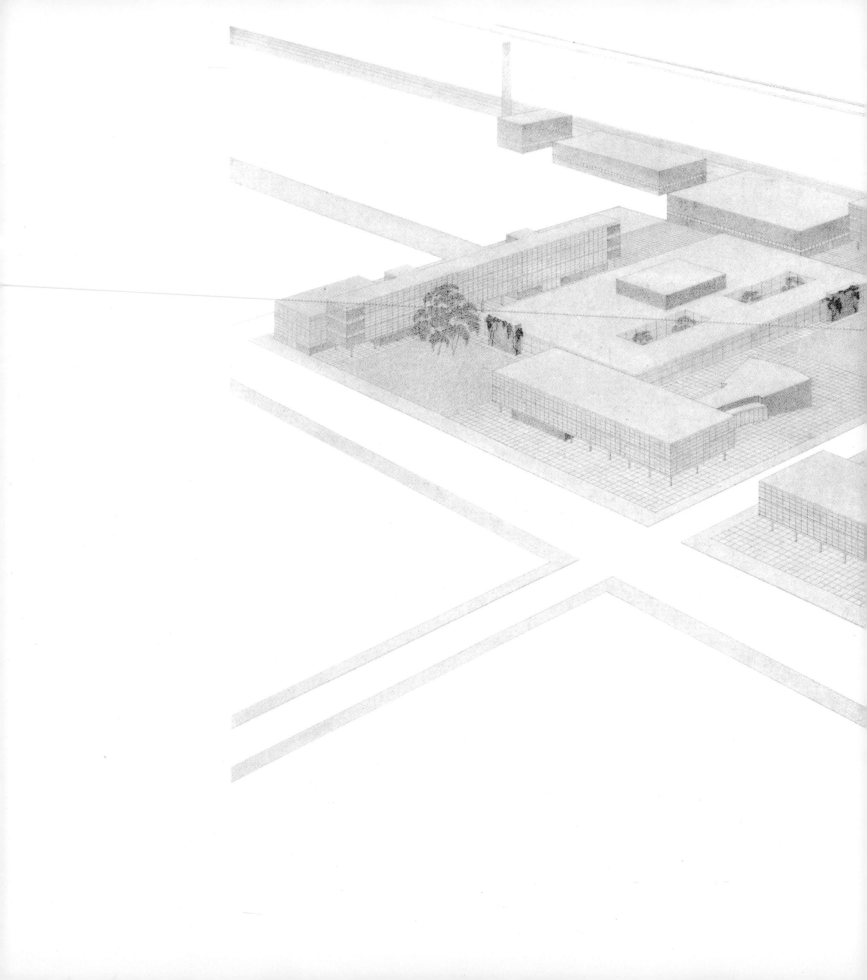

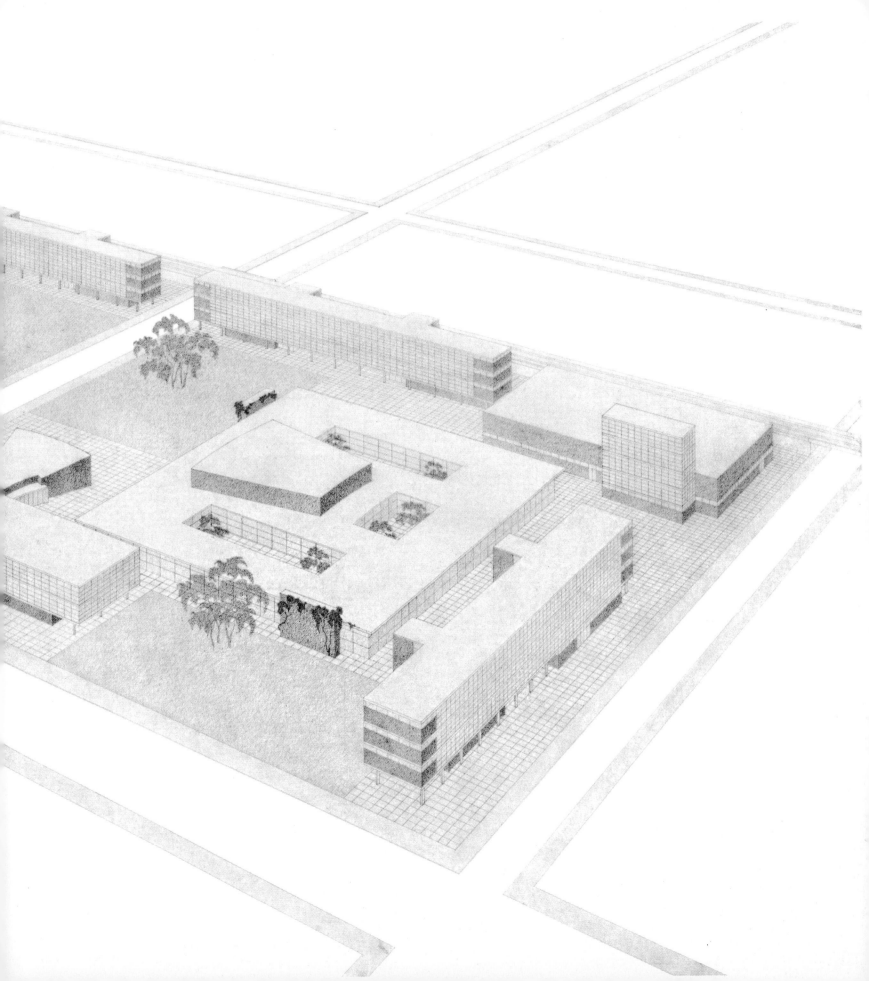

Illinois Institute of Technology (IIT), Chicago, 1938–1958
Steel-frame campus buildings

The campus of an American university is an area, complete in itself, in which classrooms, research facilities and, for some students, accommodation are provided.

A slum area had to be cleared to make way for the buildings of the new IIT campus. It was a condition imposed by the city that the existing street system should be retained. The area where the campus was to be developed was divided into a planning grid based on a 24-foot module.

Limited funds made extreme economy essential, and this is reflected in the materials and forms of construction: load-bearing brick walls, exposed reinforced concrete skeletons and pure steel skeletons filled with brick or glass. The beauty of materials and the masterly skill with which they are handled architecturally show to particular advantage in the single storey buildings where it was not necessary to fireproof the structure with concrete. The design of the classroom and laboratory blocks was based on a lucid order and structure and has not been outdated by the passage of time – although the campus took 20 years to build.

The buildings on the IIT campus are particularly clear examples of the skin and skeleton type of construction. This principle affords the greatest possible freedom in the design of the plan and facade. The load-bearing structural parts provide, as it were, the skeleton while the walls filling the gaps form the skin. The idea is in itself centuries old. Mies van der Rohe has scrutinized buildings of past stylistic eras down to their structural core.

Chemical Engineering and Metallurgy Building (IIT), 1945–1946

The program of the Chemical Engineering and Metallurgy Building called for a two-storey building five modules by twelve modules on plan (campus module 24 × 24 feet).

The structural parts of this steel-framed building are fire-proofed with concrete. The skin is stepped forward one brick length in front of the outer edge of the columns. An I-beam is welded to the column. The brick wall forming the panel is keyed in between its flanges. Outside it is flush with the front edge of the rolled steel section. At parapet height a T-section caps the wall and is tied into the centre of the top course of stretchers. The space remaining between the vertical load-bearing sections and the steel facing of the floor slab, whose surface is flush with the vertical I-beam, is closed with a glass window held in a steel frame. The steel window-frame and the panel wall are set off from the vertical I-beam and the upper edge of the steel facing of the floor slab by a visible joint. The contrast between the non-bearing wall and the bearing stanchions is particularly evident at the corner of the building.

Trees shade the glazing which runs the full length of the facade, behind which the classrooms and laboratories are located. The rooms of the teaching staff are arranged round an inner court.

The main entrance is an integral part of the facade ▷

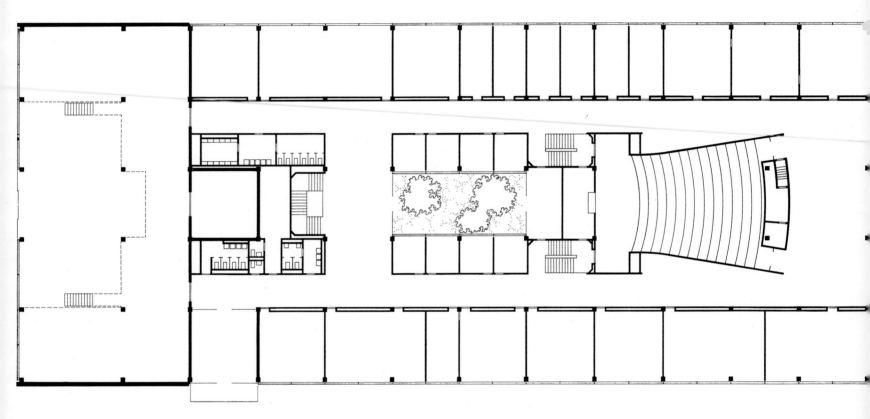

△ Plan with classrooms. Inner court and auditorium
in the centre. Scale 1:400 (1/32"=1'– 0")

Aluminium side door with swivel hinge ▷

Structure of the skeleton and texture of the ▷ ▷
brickwork

Chemistry Building (IIT), 1945
Alumni Memorial Hall (IIT), 1945

These two buildings are of fire-proof steel-frame construction. The exposed parts of the frame are painted black and the panels are filled with sand-coloured bricks and glass.

Variations in the number of floors and in the dimensions, which are always based on the module, make for harmony in the disposition of the buildings over the site plan. The trees soften the strict rhythms of the facades. Wild ivy adds a lively touch to the large areas of brick wall and forms an attractive contrast to the precision of the technical forms.

The details of the glass-and-steel skeleton buildings of IIT are more or less identical. In plan and elevation the proportions of the Alumni Memorial Hall are particularly pleasing and harmonious.

◁ Inner garden brings planting and light to the interior of the building

Pencil drawing: Alternative plan for siting buildings ▷

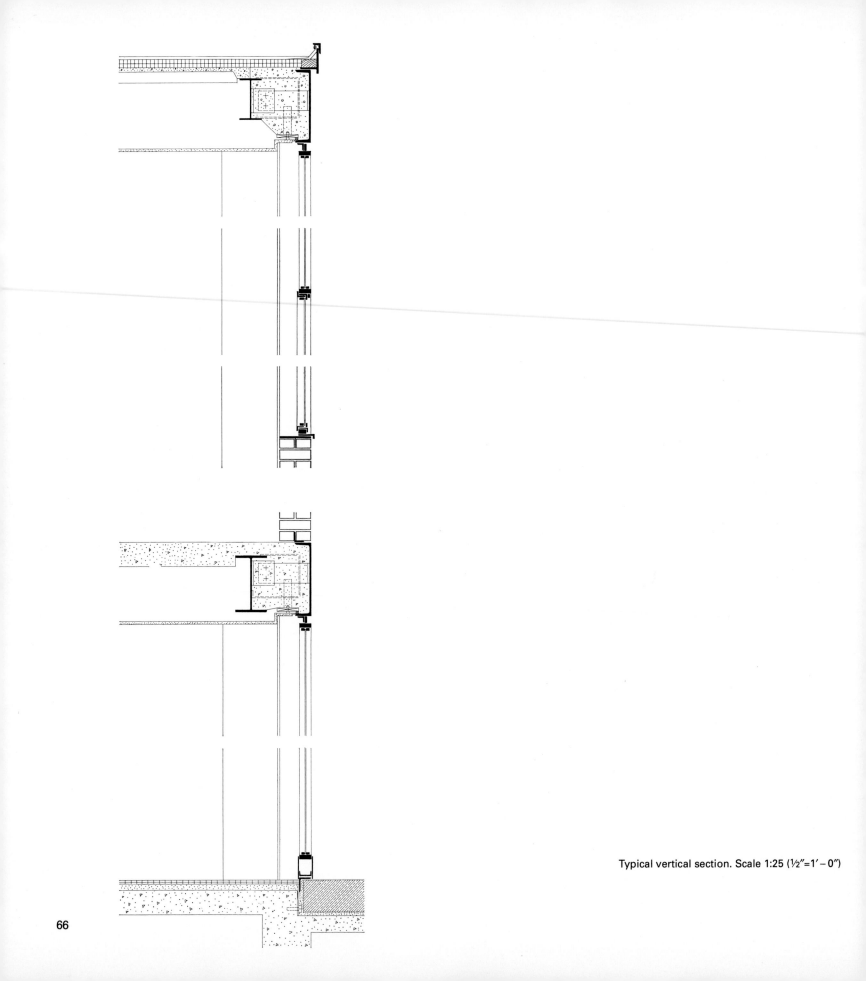

Typical vertical section. Scale 1:25 ($\frac{1}{2}''=1'-0''$)

66

◁ Brickwork slightly set back at the steel frame

Chemistry building (IIT):　　　　　　　　　▷
Symmetrical pattern of the facade

67

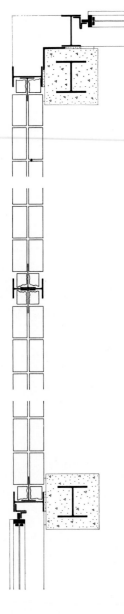

◁ Typical horizontal section.
Scale 1:25 (½″=1′–0″)

Steel frame with ivy growing over the exposed
brickwork

East facade: Structural frame and brick panels ▷

Library and Administration Building (IIT), project 1944

The most mature project among the campus buildings, unfortunately, will not be built. When Mies van der Rohe retired from teaching at the IIT, the administration no longer felt under an obligation to have the projects he had prepared carried out.

Because the library and administration was in the form of a one-storey hall the building regulation calling for a fire-proof casing over the steelwork did not apply. Features of construction, such as the transfer of loads to stanchions and the junction of surfaces of different materials, are clearly visible both inside and outside. All the constructional elements employed are subordinated to the load-bearing steel structure.

The hall is 13 modules long (312 feet) and 28 feet high. It is 192 feet wide with a column every third module. The offices along the two long sides of the hall are subdivided by means of partitions eight feet high. The book stacks of the library are enclosed from ground-level to the roof line by brick walls. A mezzanine platform – set aside for the administration – is held between four inside columns and overlooks the interior court.

The I-beam, which is a particularly prominent feature of this library, can be stressed in only one direction. This, Mies van der Rohe refers to as the Gothic principle. The column which is cruciform or star-shaped in cross-section and can be loaded in two directions is, he says, typical of the Renaissance.

Detail of the girder construction ▷

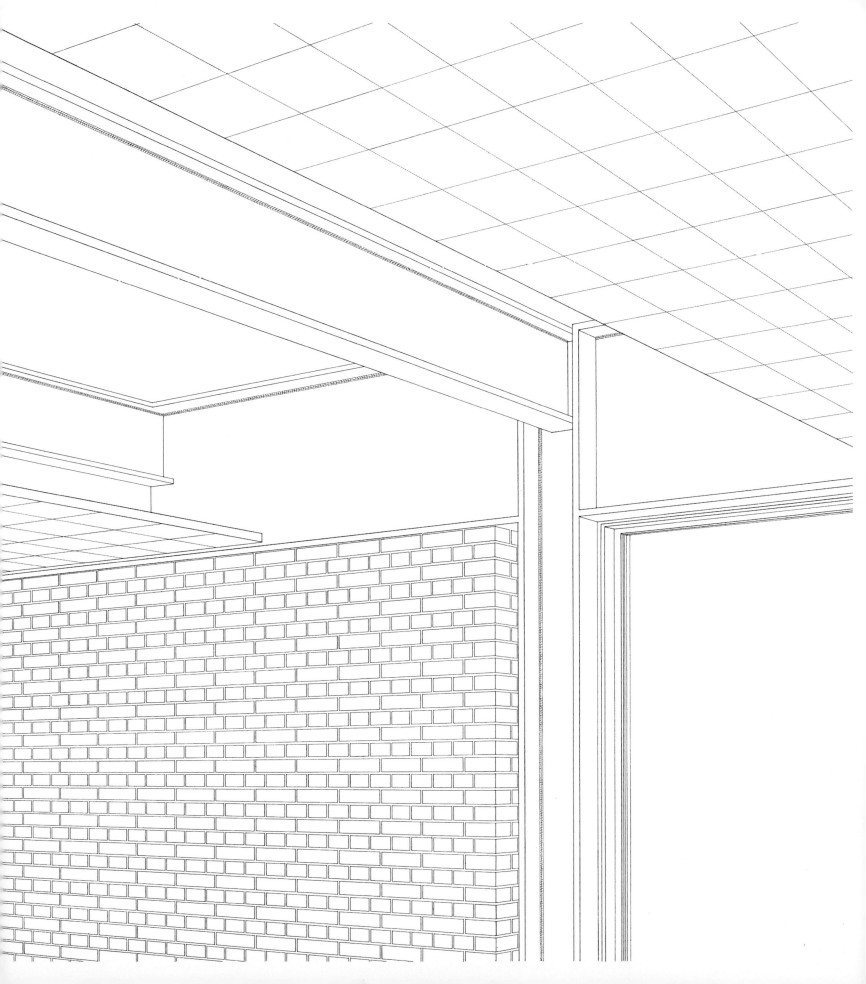

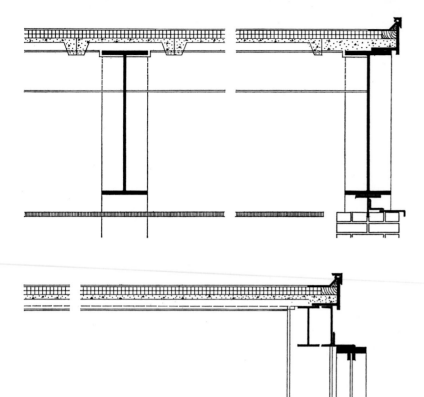

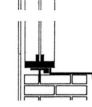

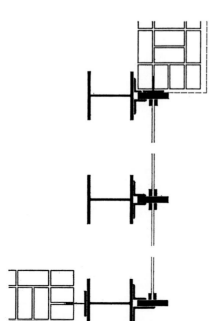

Two vertical sections and one horizontal section.
Scale 1:25 (½"=1'-0")

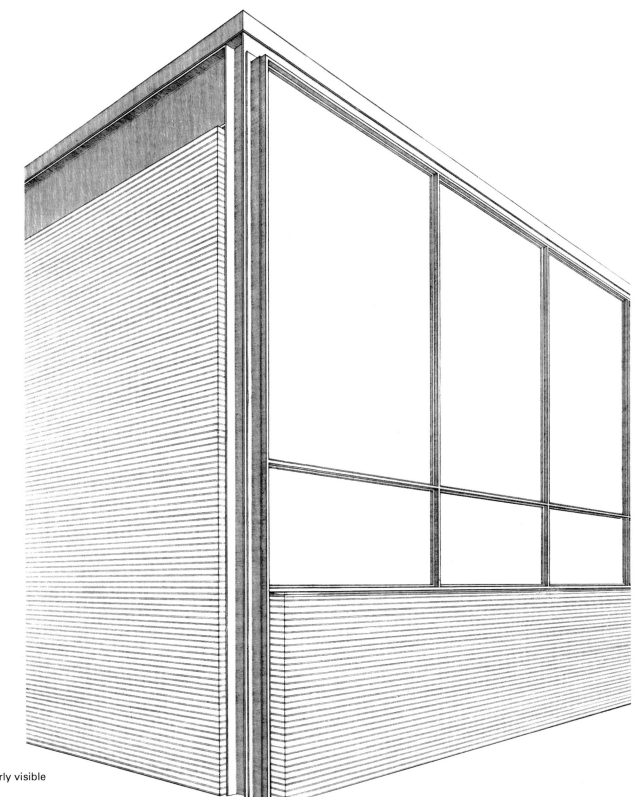

The construction and materials are clearly visible
at the corner of the building

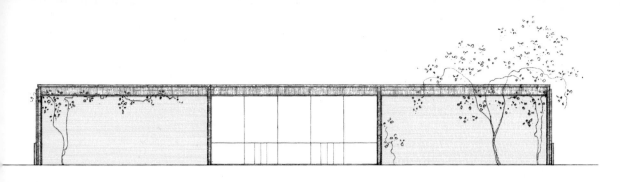

◁ Cross-sections and south and north elevation of
the administration building and library (IIT).
Scale 1:400 ($\frac{1}{32}'' = 1' - 0''$)

Front elevation and plan of the mezzanine.   ▷
Scale 1:400 ($\frac{1}{32}'' = 1' - 0''$)

Sketch showing the building in its setting   ▷ ▷

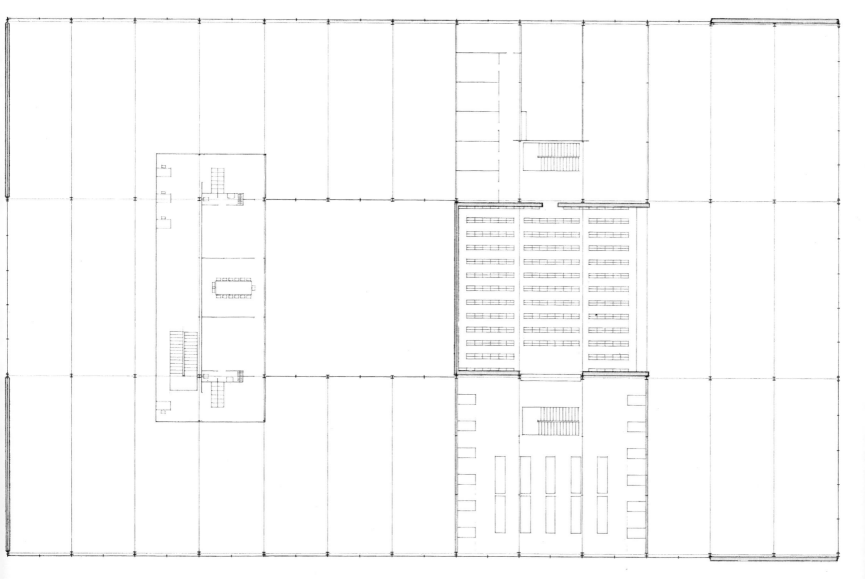

80

Truss construction with suspended roof

With the aim of providing complete flexibility of arrangement in the interior, a vast hall-like structure has been created entirely free of internal columns. The roof is suspended from a system of trusses which are supported upon outside columns, thus leaving the interior entirely unobstructed. This building simply contains a large space enclosed by the flat suspended roof and the vertical outer skin of glass. It therefore achieves the ultimate in unity of spatial, aesthetic and technological organization. Mies van der Rohe says: "Where technology attains its true fulfilment, it transcends into architecture."

This system of truss construction for large halls can serve a variety of functions. It has been employed for a school building (for architecture) and preserved in a theatre project.

Crown Hall (IIT), Architecture and Design Building, 1952–1956

This glass-and-steel hall, which is free from inside supports, provides a work centre for the students and staff of the faculty of architecture and town planning (working together in such close proximity makes for an easy relationship between students and benefits their studies). Students' work is regularly on display in the central exhibition area of the hall.

The roof of the building measures 120 × 220 feet. It is suspended from four welded plate-girders which span the entire width of the roof at 60-foot centres. At the ends the roof slab projects 20 feet beyond the outer truss. A glass-and-steel wall encloses the building. The lower panels of glass are sand-blasted; the upper windows and those at the entrance are of transparent glass; fitted on the inside above the sand-blasted glass are Venetian blinds which are kept in a down position to ensure an even distribution of light.

A monumental flight of travertine steps leads by way of a platform terrace to the main entrance level, which is six feet above the ground. The white acoustic ceiling is 18 feet above the terrazzo floor. The free-standing partitions are of oak.

Post and beam as structural elements

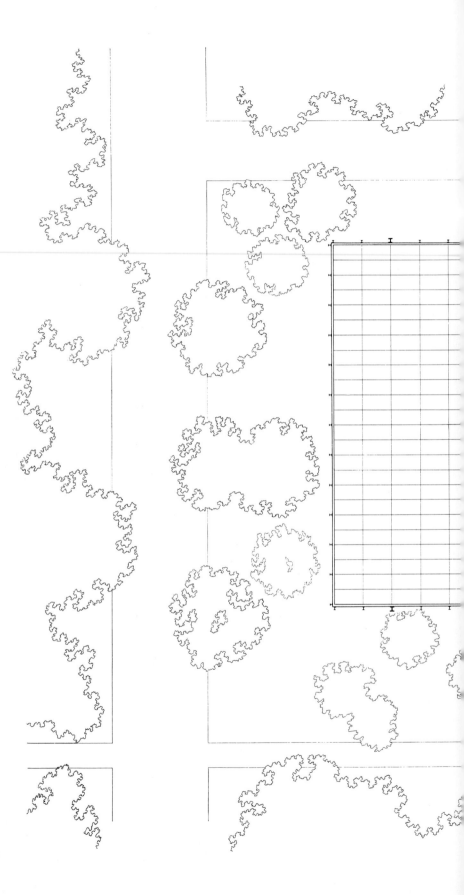

General plan of Crown Hall.
Scale 1:400 (1/32"=1' – 0")

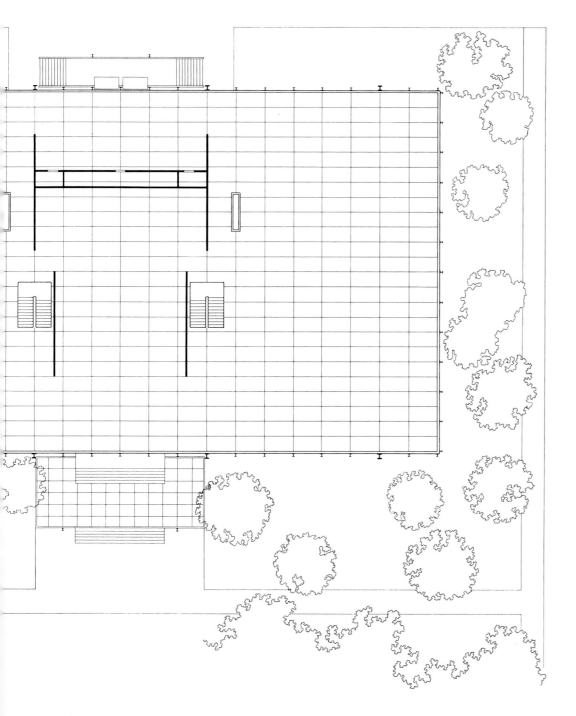

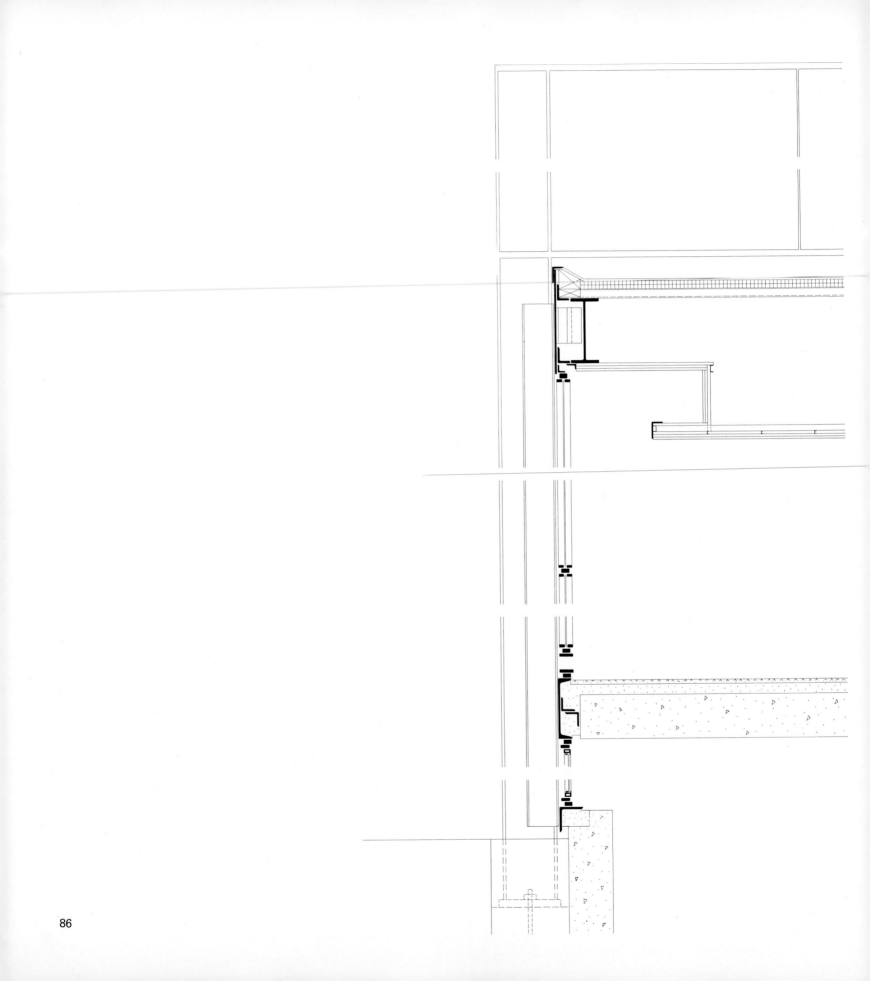

◁ Vertical section. Scale 1:25 (½″=1′– 0″)

Four steel trusses carry the roof ▷

Acacias surround the glass-and-steel building. ▷ ▷
The architect provides the structure and adds
creative embellishments

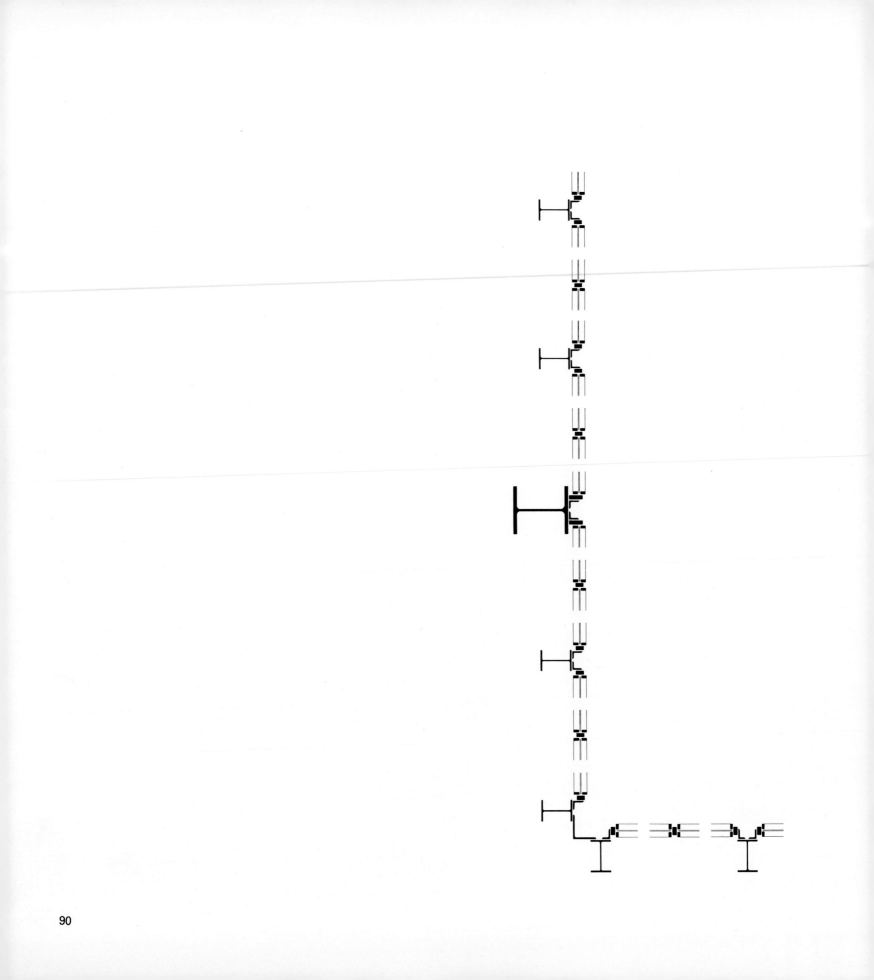

◁ Horizontal section. Scale 1:25 (½″=1′ – 0″)

View looking out through the main entrance ▷

Steps and pedestal in travertine

◁ Typical movable wall in wood

Partitioning the interior makes a harmonious   ▷
pattern

The facade is the same inside and outside
(sun blinds, transparent glass, opal glass)

National Theatre Mannheim, competition 1952–1953

This building consists of a low, transparent hall in which are accommodated a large theatre for 1,300 persons and a small theatre for 500 persons.

Visitors enter the building by way of the ground floor which is four metres high and set back about eight metres from the facade. The walls, which are faced with marble, seem to flow through the building. The upper floor is twelve metres high and houses two seating areas, a portion of the larger being cantilevered into the auditorium. The stages share a common area in the centre.

The roof slab, which is 160 metres long, is suspended from seven lattice trusses which span the 80 metres of the site at centres of 24 metres. The enclosing wall is of steel and glass.

The outer integument is carried by lattice girders. ▷
Inside, the cantilevered balcony can be seen

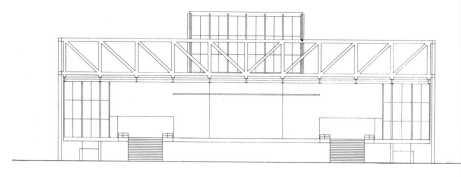

△ Section of the Mannheim theatre.
Scale 1:800 (1/64″=1′–0″)

Longitudinal section and plan.   ▷
Scale 1:800 (1/64″=1′–0″)

Model showing general appearance of the   ▷ ▷
building. Technology leaves the construction
plain for all to see

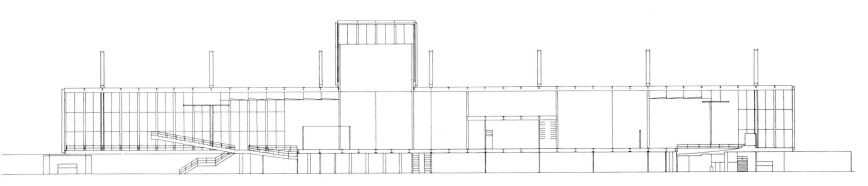

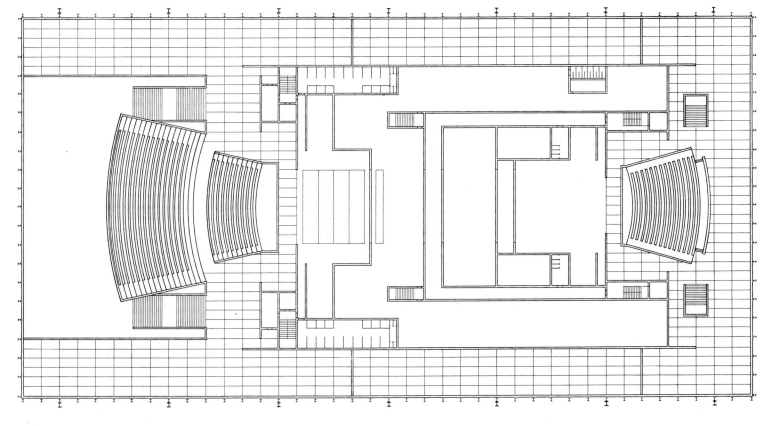

Glass houses with a steel frame

The columns are located outside so as to give infinite flexibility in internal arrangement. The construction of the roof slab depends on whether the columns are arranged along the two long sides of the house or all round its perimeter.

The use of steel and glass gives an uninterrupted view of the natural surroundings and enables the interior space to be projected outside. A pedestal or terrace in front of the building fits the house into the environment with a sense of belonging.

These steel-and-glass structures are set amidst the luxuriance of nature like crystals. Only the art of omission reveals the true structure of a building and reduces it to elements of pure beauty and pure spirit.

Farnsworth House, a single-room glass house, Plano (Illinois), 1945–1950

This week-end house with an all-one-room first floor stands on a flat meadow between tall leafy trees. The living side faces the Fox River, which forms the southern limit of the site.

The roof and floor slab are raised above the ground by eight outside steel columns and enclosed by a glass skin. An inner core of natural primavera wood containing the service installations partitions off the kitchen, sleeping and living areas.

A raised terrace in front of the house forms a link with the lawn. The various levels are joined by two flights of steps. The steps, the terrace and the floor are faced with travertine slabs measuring 2×3 feet. All exposed steel elements are painted white. The transparent sheets of glass can be screened by curtains of natural-coloured shantung. The dimensions of the house are 77×29 feet. The pedestal measures 55×22 feet and the interior is 9.50 feet high. The columns are placed 22 feet apart.

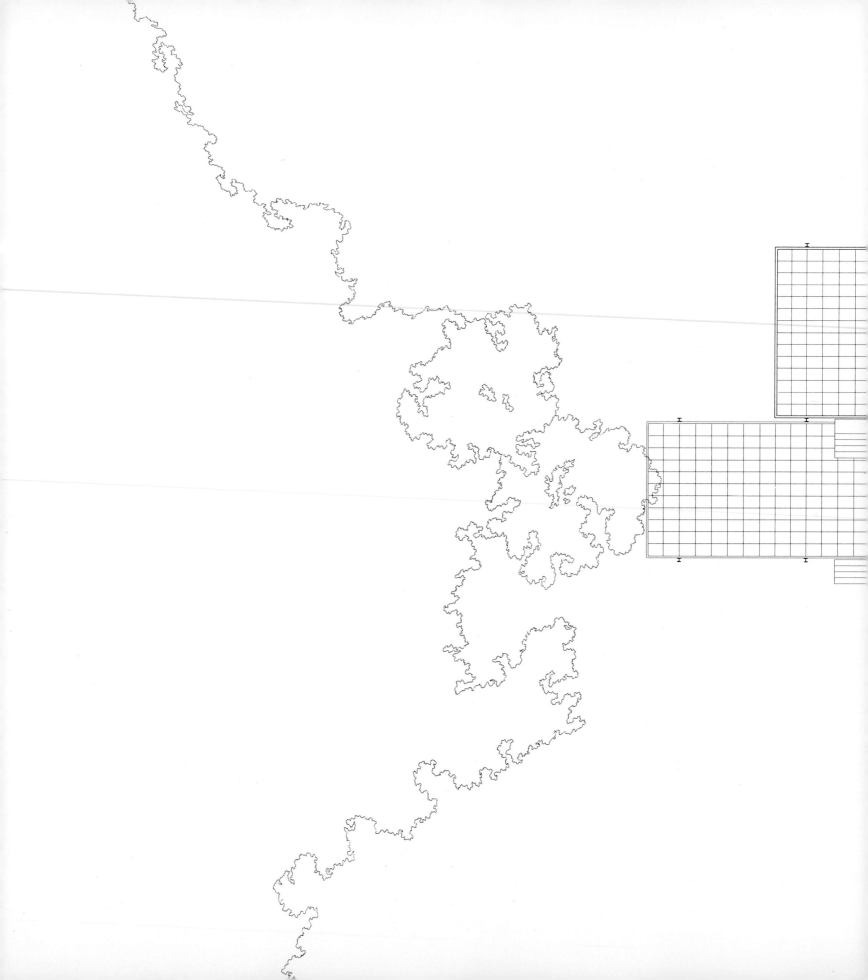

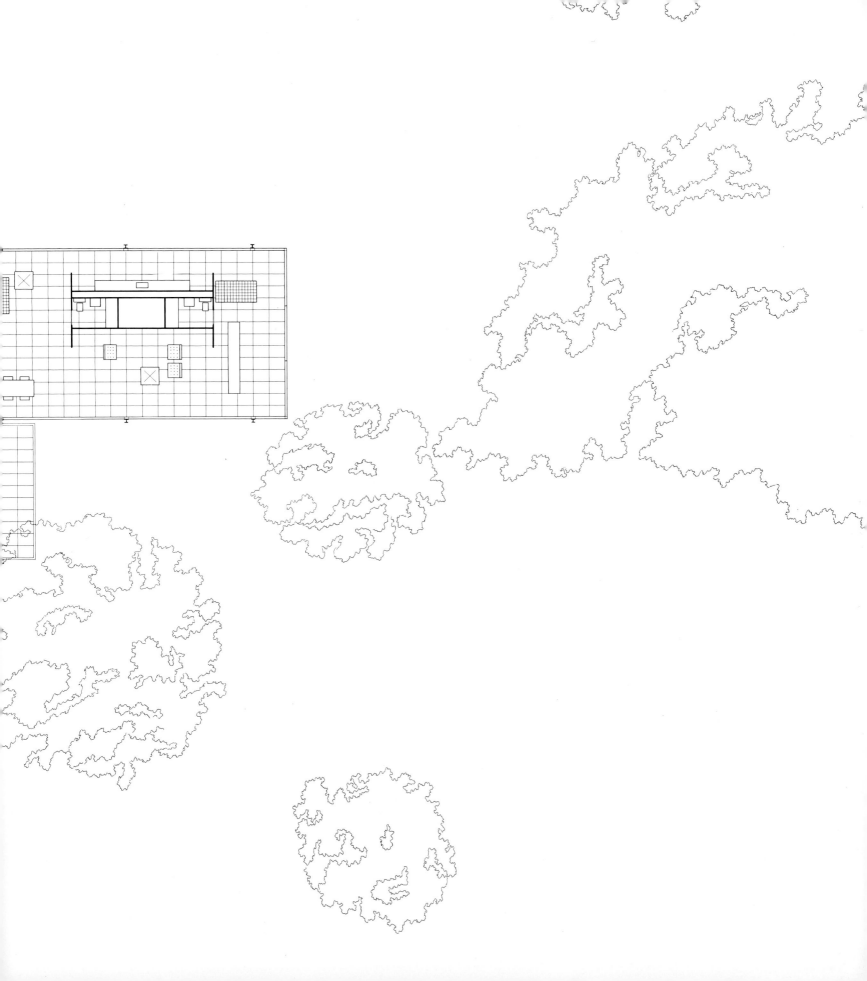

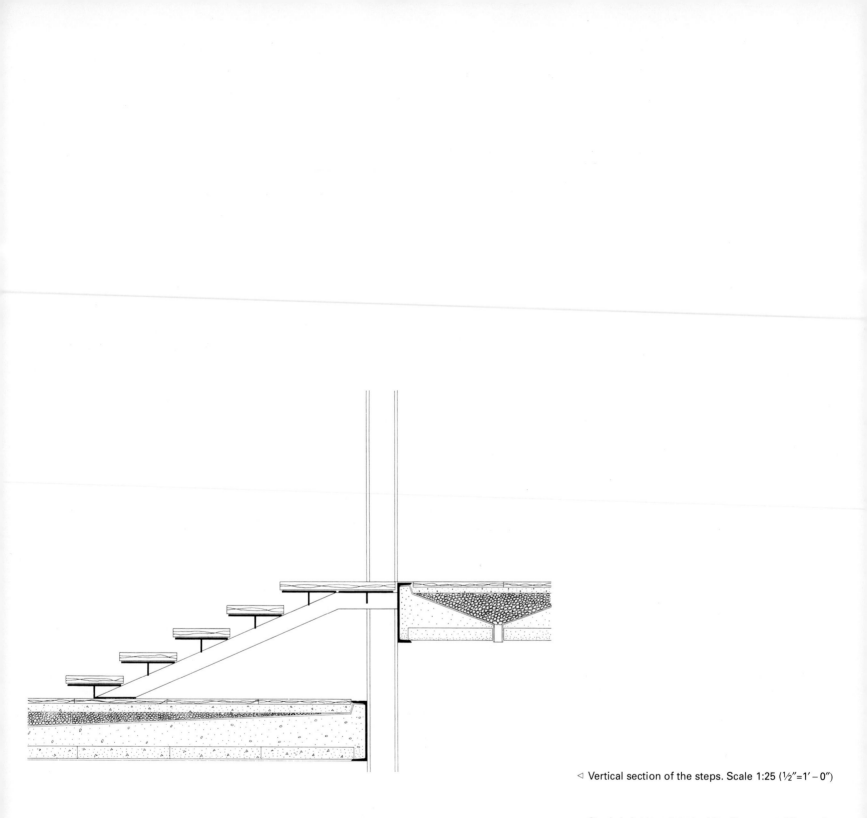

◁ Vertical section of the steps. Scale 1:25 (½″=1′ – 0″)

Steel skeleton painted white. Terrace and floor of ▷
travertine slabs. Curtains of natural shantung

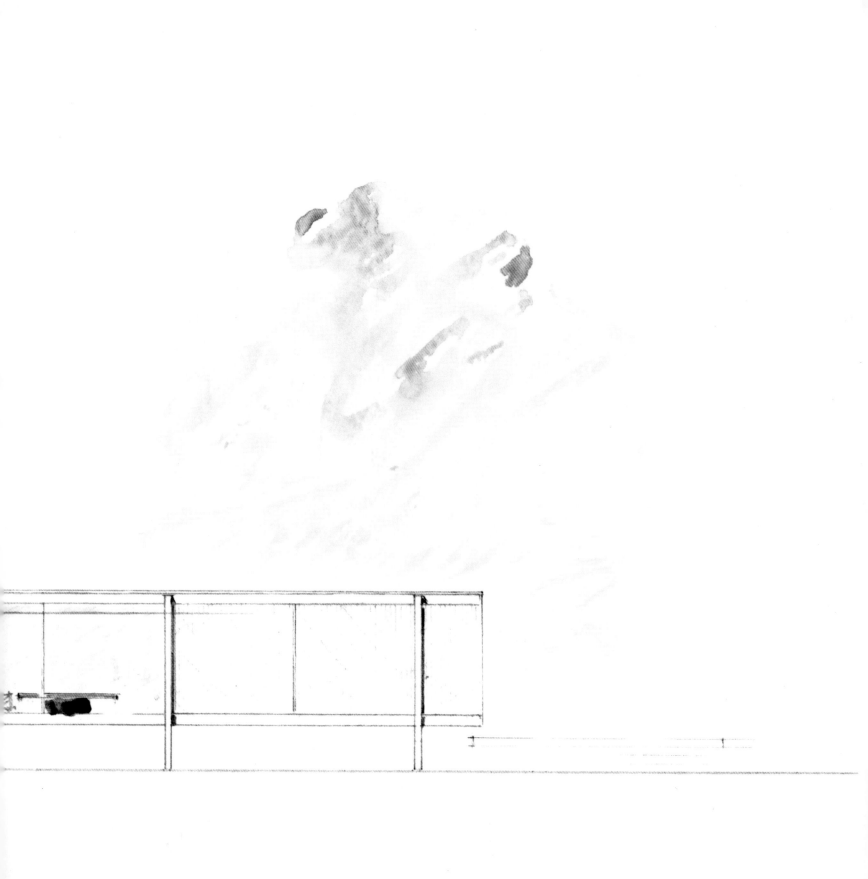

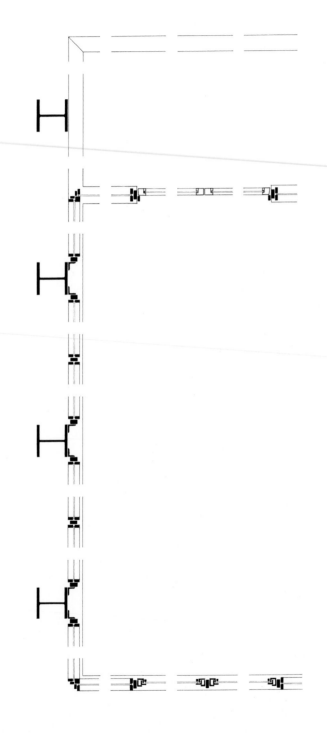

◁ Horizontal section. Scale 1:25 (½″=1′ – 0″)

The architecture provides a frame for nature.   ▷
Inside and outside are unified. A fine netting is
spread to keep out mosquitoes

The building is raised above ground level. The   ▷ ▷
ceiling and floor are held between eight columns.
The building is enclosed with glass

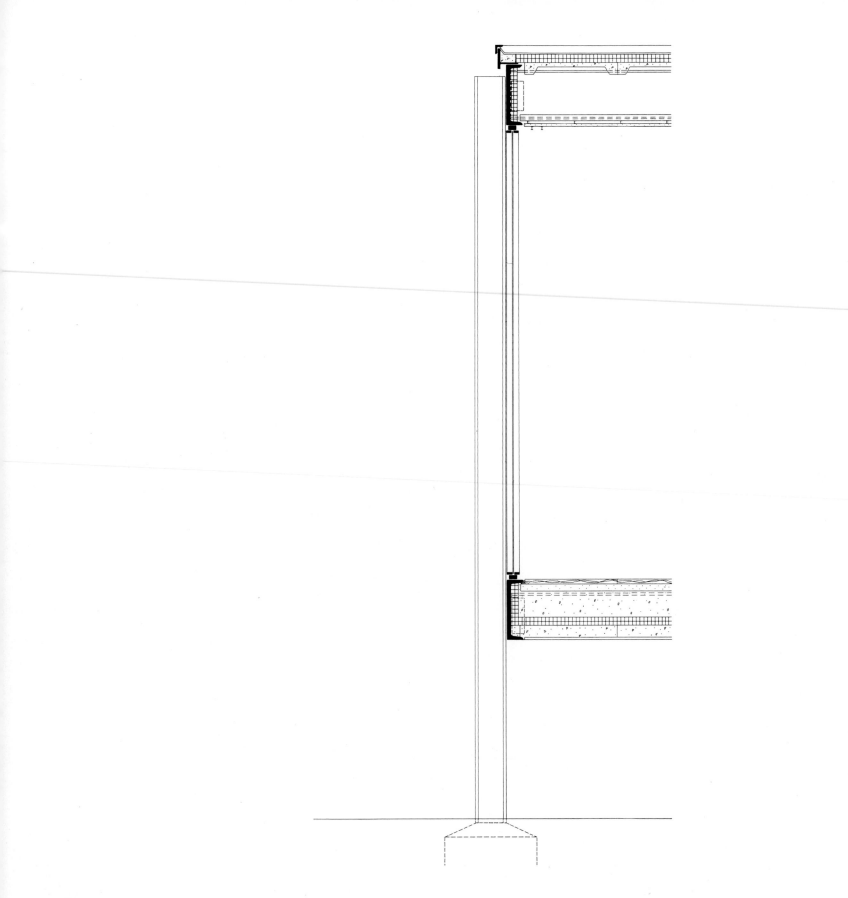

◁ Vertical section. Scale 1:25 (½″=1′– 0″)

Detail of standard T-beam column and cornice　　▷

Caine House, multi-room glass house, project 1950

This project was the solution to a building programme comprising a variety of needs at a high level of luxury. The different zones for family life are accommodated under a roof slab measuring 48 × 110 feet, and supported on twelve steel columns. The floor is of stone slabs planned on a module of 3 × 5 feet and extends outside to form a terrace. A glass wall around the perimeter separates the interior and exterior.

The service rooms and the servants' bedrooms, together with the children's playrooms, are separated from the main part of the house, where free-standing screens divide up the space into living and sleeping areas for the family and guests.

General plan of a multi-room glass house: Service ▷ room on right, large living area in centre and left wing. Scale 1:200 (¹⁄₁₆"=1'–0")

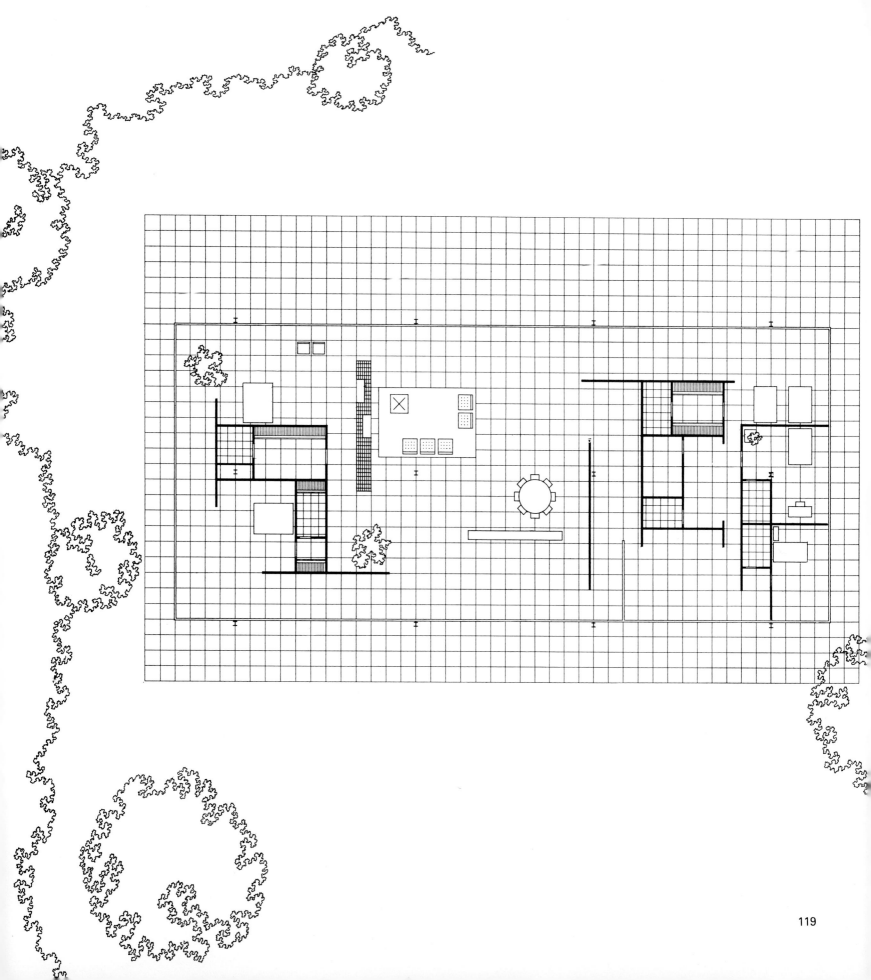

119

Glass house with four columns, project 1950–1951

A square room is open to nature on all four sides. The roof slab is the only visible horizontal element and appears to hover over the low partition walls.

The rigid roof slab measuring 50 × 50 feet is a grid welded together from square steel sections and is supported on four visible columns standing in the centre of each side. Set aside from the centre, a core containing the plumbing separates the service from the living area.

The basic idea was to situate a house so that it was open in all directions to the surrounding landscape. It is a pavilion in a garden and like the court houses is separated from the road by a brick wall screen.

General plan of glass house with four columns: ▷
Large terrace in front. Scale 1:200 (1/16″=1′–0″)

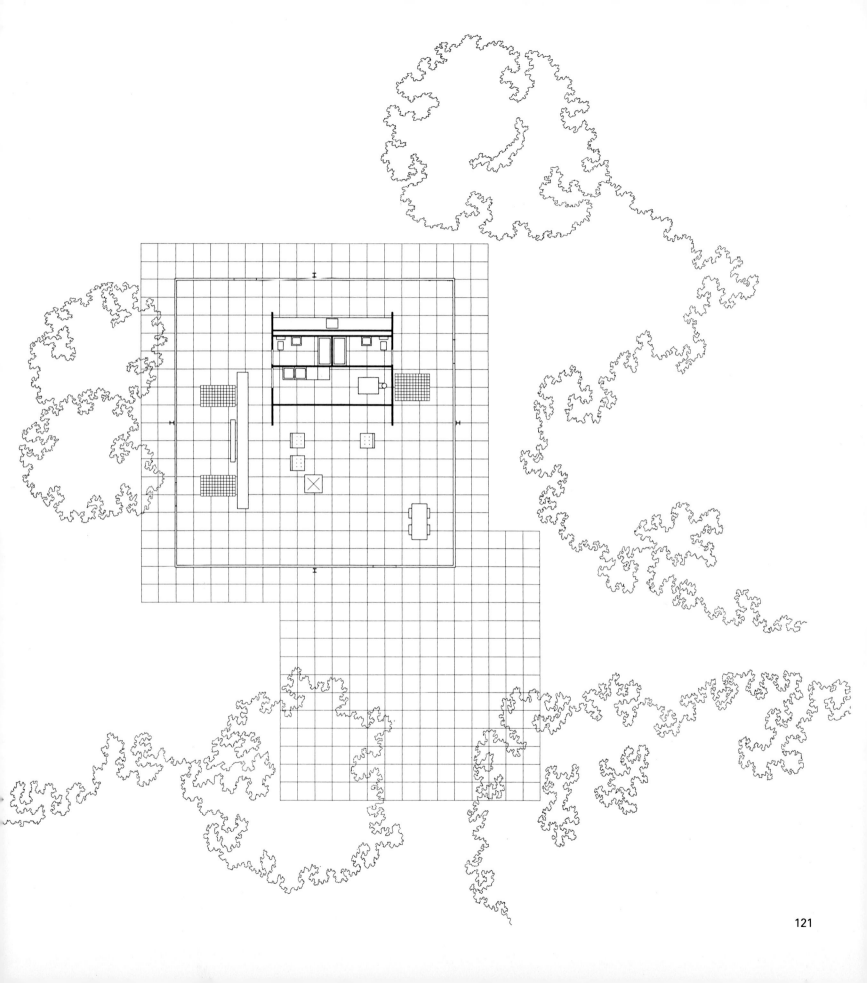

Steel-and-glass apartment towers

The first tower blocks of apartments were executed in reinforced concrete. A drawing of the facade in steel and glass showed the way to erecting tower blocks as steel-framed buildings. These buildings are the fruition of a quarter of a century's reflection. By day and by night their proportions, their patterning and their glass walls make a vivid impression.

The outside sections of rolled steel or extruded aluminium containing the glass form a vigorously articulated main facade. Since there are no visual limits to space as seen from inside the apartment, the occupants enjoy an entirely new experience of their environment, feeling liberated and detached from the earth.

At the 860 Lake Shore Drive Apartments the I-beams were welded directly to the steel plates which cover the exterior of the fireproofed steel frame. Thus the load-bearing columns and the floor spandrels become visible on the face of the building. At the 900 Esplanade Apartments and the Commonwealth Promenade Apartments, on the other hand, the window units are placed in front of the structural frame.

Promontory Apartments, Chicago, 1946–1949

This 22-storey framed apartment tower stands on the southern stretch of Lake Shore Drive overlooking Lake Michigan.

The structure is of exposed reinforced concrete with brick panels. The reinforced concrete columns are stepped back progressively towards the upper storeys as the loads decrease. The sketches record the development: the first drawing shows a concrete version with the brick filled panels; the second shows the application of a steel-and-glass skin.

The steel-and-glass version was developed with the intention of giving the interior greater openness and was used in later tower projects. Mies van der Rohe's umcompromising discipline behind the development the purely skeletal building carries the tradition of the Chicago School forward.

Promontory Apartments. Reinforced concrete
version with columns decreasing towards the top
of the building

Steel-and-glass version. The unfolding of the curtain wall

860 Lake Shore Drive Apartments, Chicago, 1948–1951

Lake Shore Drive with its eight traffic lanes runs on the Lake Michigan side of these two apartment towers. The towers are set with their long sides at right angles to each other, their orientation being determined by the city road grid.

The 26 apartment floors are carried by a steel skeleton which had to be fire-proofed with concrete. The columns are placed 21 feet apart in both directions, dividing the narrow side of the rectangular plan into three bays and the long side into five bays. The structural expression is achieved by making the steel-finished floor beams and the outer columns run flush with the surface of the glass and thus form the outer skin. The I-beam mullions run the full height of the building at 5'-3" centres.

The contrast between the glass surfaces and the black structure of the skin is underlined by blinds of a uniform pale colour. Floor-to-ceiling glazing projects the daily pageant of nature into the interior. Each storey from floor to ceiling is 8.50 feet high. Both towers contain apartments of several rooms arranged on an open plan. The ground floor is 17 feet high and is completely glazed. Slabs of travertine run through the entrance hall and its surrounds and connect the two buildings.

The two apartment towers with 26 ▷
storeys. The structure is enclosed
with steel and glass on all sides

The four glass towers on Lake ▷ ▷
Michigan. 900 Esplanade Apartments on right with grey-tinted
glass wall

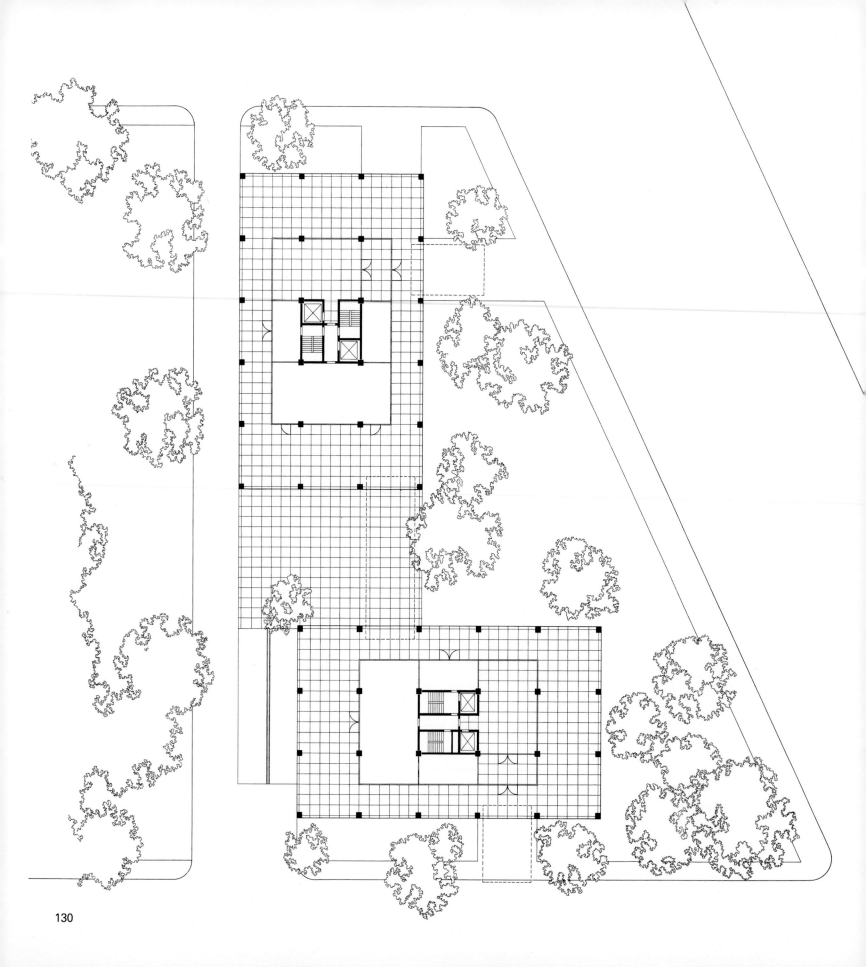

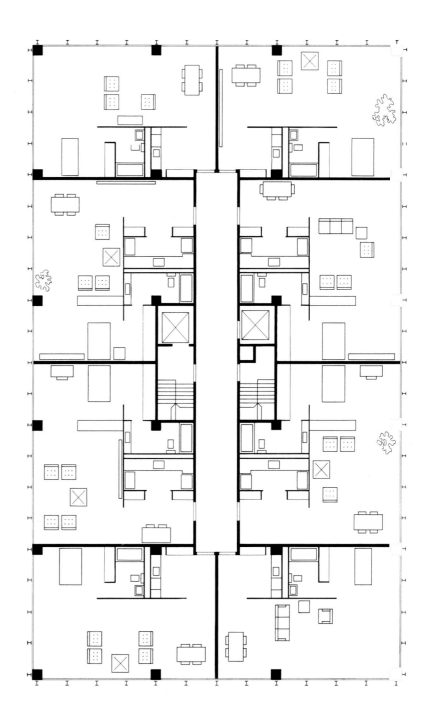

◁ General plan of 860 Lake Shore Drive Apartments.
In front of the apartments is the expressway and
Lake Michigan. Scale 1:400 (1/32″=1′ – 0″)

Uncompromising all-one-room plan (not   ▷
executed). Scale 1:200 (1/16″=1′ – 0″)

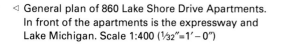

Glass runs the full width of the facade. Uniform   ▷ ▷
grey curtains. Aluminium window frames.
Structural parts painted black for contrast

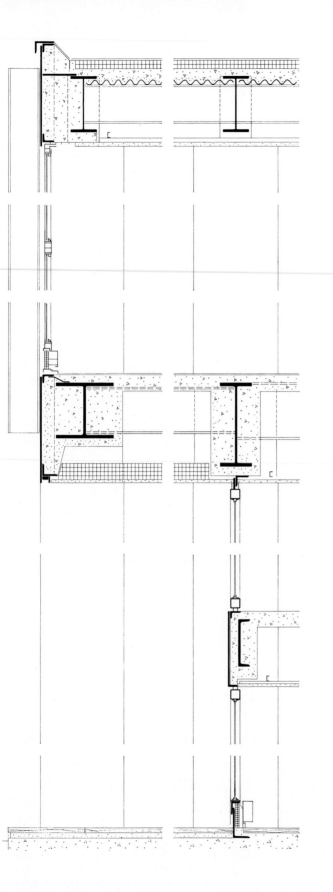

◁ Vertical section. Scale 1:25 (½″=1′–0″)

Recessed fully-glazed lobby ▷

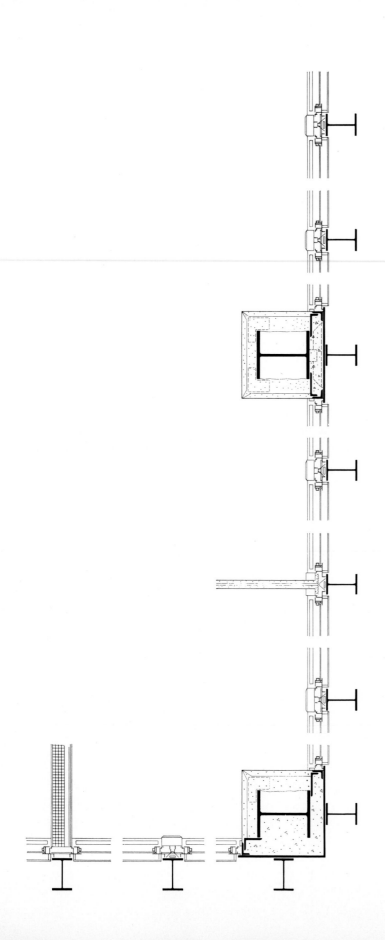

◁ Horizontal section. Scale 1:25 (½″=1′ – 0″)

The T-beams soar skywards   ▷

Commonwealth Promenade Apartments, Chicago, 1953–1956

Economic and air-conditioning factors led to further design developments after the 860 Lake Shore Drive Apartment scheme.

Since economy dictated the use of reinforced concrete flat slab construction, a non-load-bearing skin of extruded aluminium and glass was developed to hang in front of the concrete frame. This system of enclosure yields windows of equal size and provides a suitable space between the concrete column and the skin mullions for air-conditioning pipes. The columns, which grow progressively larger towards the bottom where the load to be borne increases, can be seen only in the interior and do not affect the curtain wall.

Grey-tinted glass and black aluminium was used for the 900 Lake Shore Apartments whereas in all the other tower projects the aluminium was left in its natural silver-grey colour.

Junction of two curtain walls of aluminium sections

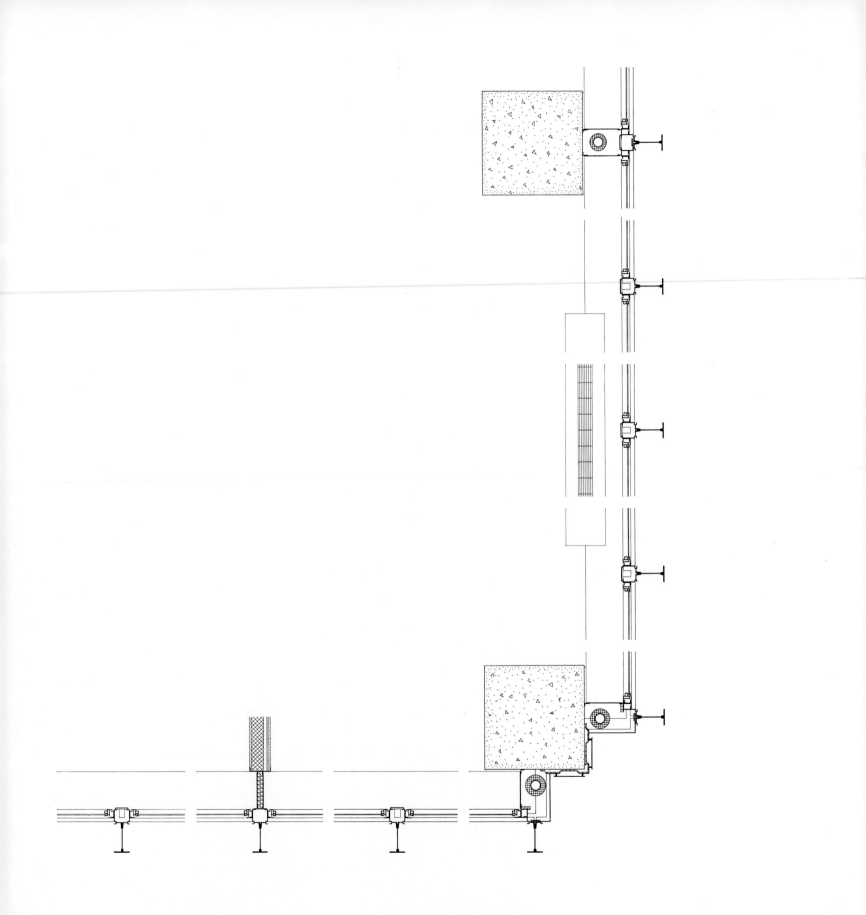

◁ Horizontal section. Scale 1:25 (½"=1' – 0")

Elements of the curtain wall showing
structural joint ▷

The steel-and-glass apartment building now evolved a stage further to produce a new type of office building, a type which has set a trend all over the world. The remarkable skill with which he handles the steel-and-glass skeleton allows Mies van der Rohe to display his mastery in the rhythmic patterning of the facade and the use he makes of his materials. After the structure has been clarified, attention is turned to the refinements. A particularly good example is provided by the Seagram Building, where bronze and tinted glass lend the soaring steel skeleton building a magical effect.

In the low rise offices for Friedrich Krupp in Essen and Bacardi in Mexico City, the steel-and-glass structure is articulated with a lively delicacy: the principle of order and regularity permeating the whole is made apparent down to the smallest detail. Nothing is accessory: every detail serves the whole.

Mies van der Rohe readily makes reference to what is quintessential in the structure of classic edifices; timeless buildings embody the spirit of their times in that each tests the limits of what can be attained through material and construction.

Seagram Administration Building, New York, 1954–1958

This 39-storey tower block of offices on Park Avenue in the centre of Manhattan's business quarter is set back 90 feet from the Park Avenue building line and soars high above a plaza bounded by the main street and two side streets and containing two pools with benches where passers-by can relax. Setting back the building in this way seems to detach it from surrounding structures.

The steel frame of the building is enclosed above the 24-foot-high ground floor by a curtain wall of bronze and bronze-tinted glass. The bronze gives the building a striking dignity. The materials on the ground floor are: granite slabs for the floors and terrace, slabs of travertine around the lift shafts, and bronze as an encasement for the columns. The offices are nine feet high. The columns are spaced at 28-foot intervals in every direction with six window units to each 28-foot bay. Partitions for the office rooms can be arranged behind each mullion.

The Seagram Administration Building was designed in association with Philip Johnson.

◁ The building is set back from Park Avenue

General plan of the Seagram Administration ▷
Building showing surrounding office buildings.
Scale 1:800 (1/64″=1′ – 0″)

Outer skin of bronze and tinted glass ▷ ▷

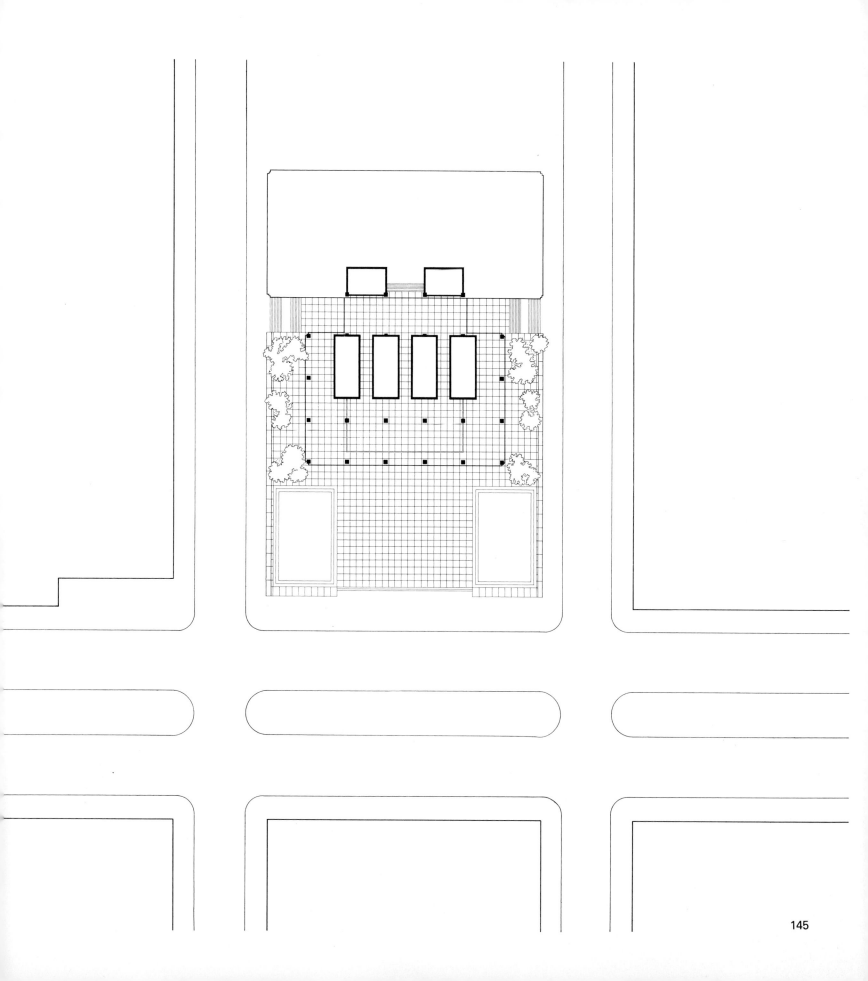

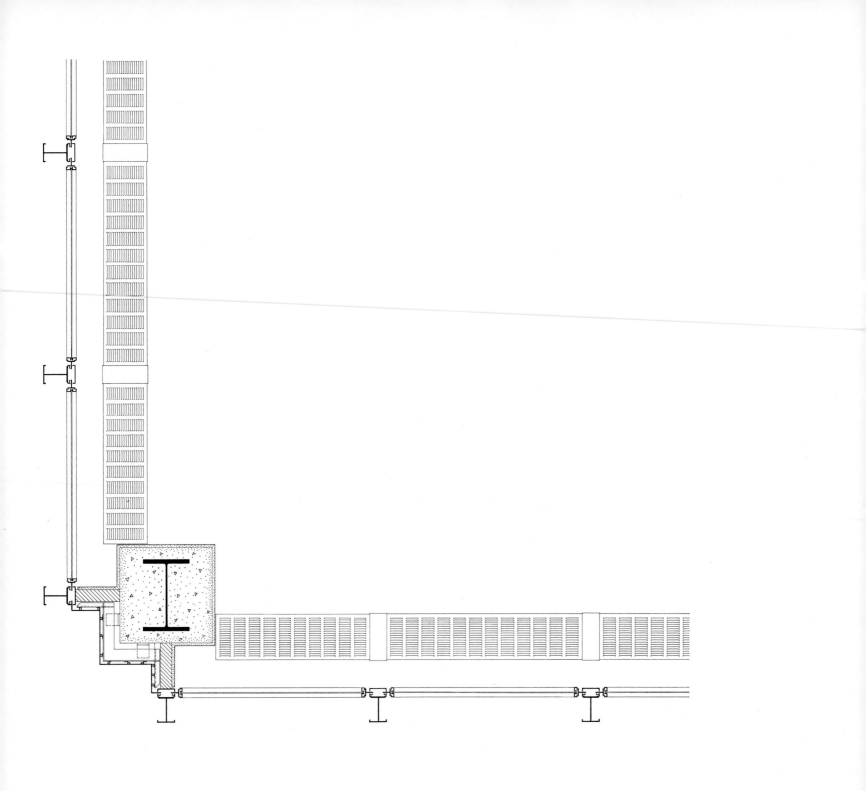

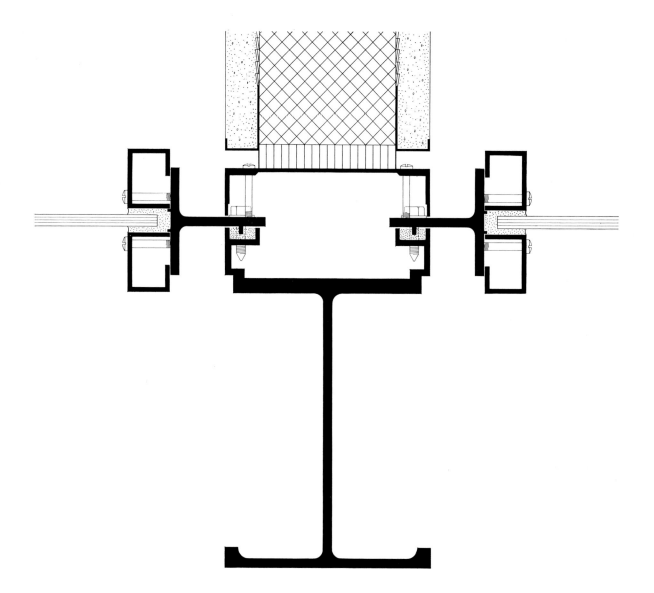

◁ Horizontal section. Scale 1:25 (½″=1′–0″)

Typical joint between bronze sections and the   △
fast-sheet window-frames. Scale 1:5 (2″=1′–0″)

◁ Rough sketch of plaza with symmetrically arranged sculptures

Spatial arrangement of entrance section ▷
with rear buildings

◁ Not the invention of forms, but imagination in construction

Corner pillar sheathed in bronze   ▷

The beauty of the travertine wall is revealed

154

Bacardi Administration Building, Mexico City, 1958–1961

The low administration building forms the entrance to the rum distillery of the Bacardi company. It consists of a single-storey hall which is raised three metres above ground level so that the body of the building is above the nearby raised highway.

The entrance hall is set back from the facade and completely glazed while, above, the floor of the office storey is opened to form a well in the centre. Two symmetrically arranged stairs connect the hall with ground level. Floor and ceiling slabs are supported by exposed columns spaced at intervals of nine metres in both directions. The total height of the building is eight metres on a plan measuring 56 × 27 metres. At the narrow ends the office storey is cantilevered 3.50 metres out beyond the last row of columns.

The steel frame and the outer columns are painted black, and the floors are of travertine. The enclosing wall is of steel and grey-tinted glass. Free-standing panel walls form cores to accommodate the service installations and partition the office spaces on the upper floor.

The interposed staircase and its symmetrically ▷ arranged counterpart lead to the office floor

General plan of the Bacardi Building and main ▷ ▷ floor. Scale 1:200 (1/16"=1'–0")

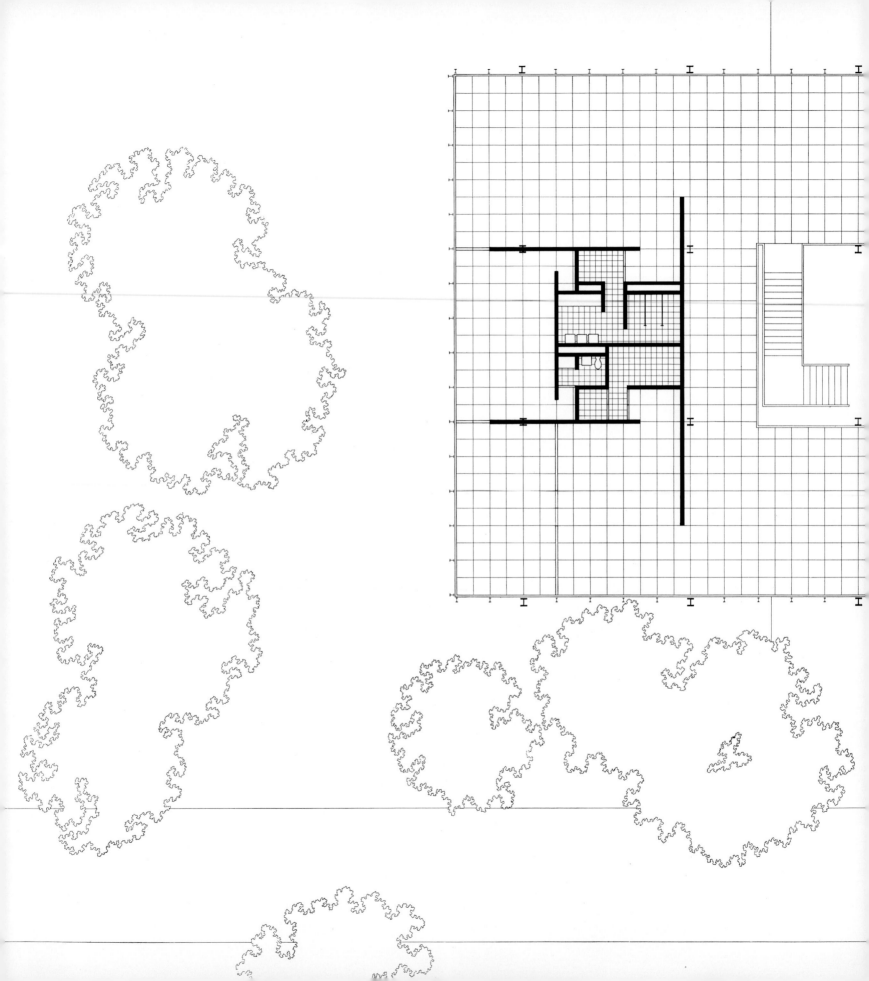

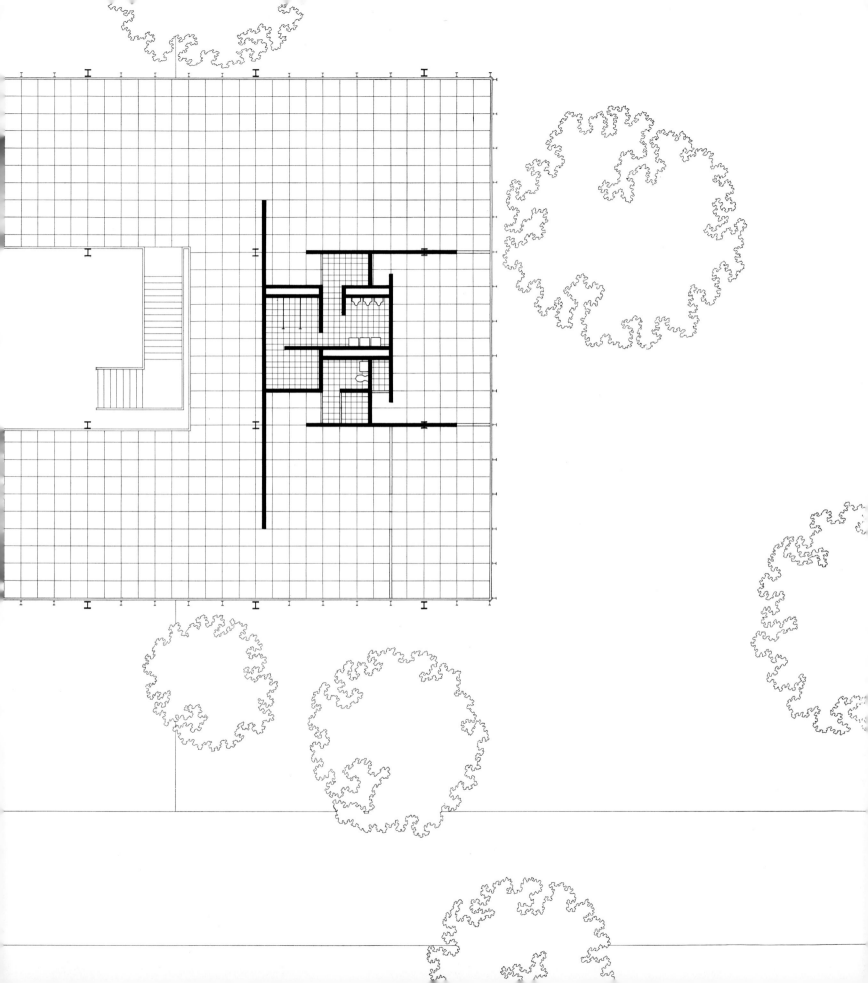

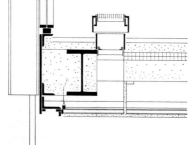

◁ Vertical section. Scale 1:25 (½″=1′ – 0″)

The steel skeleton is visible both inside and outside ▷

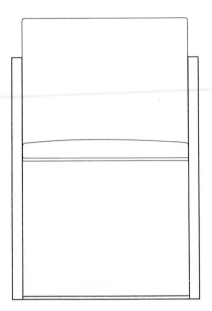

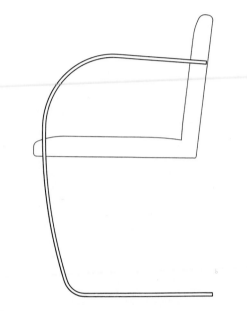

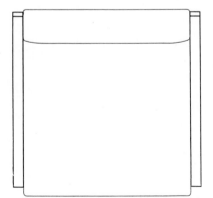

◁ Bruno chair. Scale 1:12½ (1″=1′–0″)

Panelled walnut wall in the conference room. ▷
Chairs based on the Brno model (1930)

Krupp Administration Building "Auf dem Hügel", Essen,
project 1960–1963

A granite-paved terrace on a tree-covered hill forms the base of this
strongly horizontal building. A glazed entrance lobby in the centre
of the building connects with the two office floors, which are raised
five metres above ground level. The ground floor is open and
affords views of planted inner courts and the surrounding country-
side. A spacious plaza accents the main entrance on the front. A
lower level accommodates restaurants (which open on to outside
terraces) and parking and service facilities.

The structure of the building consists of a fire-proofed steel frame
planned on a 12.80 metre square bay. The skin is of painted steel
and grey-tinted plate glass with mullions at 3.20 centres (the building's module). The offices, which are 3.10 metres from floor to
ceiling, are planned on either side of a central access corridor. The
partitions between offices are designed to be movable.

General plan of Krupp Building. Scale 1:1,000   ▷
(1/80"= 1'–0")

Two inner courts give a lively accent to the   ▷ ▷
building. In spite of the prefabricated facade
elements there is no monotony

City-planning

In these schemes, which embrace single-storey court houses, two-storey row houses and glass towers, people can find the accommodation best suited to their needs. Mies van der Rohe said: "Towns are instruments of life. They have to serve life. They are to be measured in terms of life and planned for life."

A high density of population is unavoidable, but it is made tolerable by verdant zones, Mies van der Rohe's steel-and-glass structures and, above all, by a clear layout of circulation routes for all occupants.

Lafayette Park, Detroit, 1955–1963

The layout of the park was the outcome of a collaboration between Mies van der Rohe and the city planner Ludwig Hilberseimer. Tall apartment towers and one- and two-storey terrace houses form a complete district within a large city. The park has a ring road round it with access roads routed so as to leave a traffic-free verdant zone in the centre as a play and recreation area. Parking areas are under grade.

The reflecting glass surfaces of the terrace houses disappear almost entirely into the tops of the trees, from which only the apartment towers emerge. By concentrating population in a small area the apartment towers enable generous stretches of lawn to be left for recreation.

◁ Brick walls enclose the court houses

The dangerous road is under grade ▷

Court houses as seen from the apartment towers ▷ ▷

◁ Traffic-free roads lead to the two-storey terrace houses

The lawns and planting are interposed between the ▷ towers and lower buildings

Children at play in the outdoor area ▷ ▷

Hall construction with a wide-span roof

Since it is the structure that determines the essential character of a building by Mies van der Rohe, he can design monumental hall buildings which are masterpieces of engineering and yet display an exquisite aesthetic sensibility. A wide-span roof supported only on outside columns yields a free space in which the creative imagination can be given full play. The freedom provided by a static structure is the essence of Mies van der Rohe's work. This "static" structure is, as it were, the instrument on which his creative genius can play the "dynamic" variations of his designs.

Mies van der Rohe does not build palaces, or heavy, massive fortresses. For a minimum of mass, his buildings yield a maximum in cultivated living. "Living in a state of freedom."

Convention Hall, Chicago, project 1953–1954

The Convention Hall was planned for a site near the centre of Chicago within easy reach of all transport facilities. It would be a multi-purpose hall with seating accommodation for 50,000 persons. A column-free interior would meet every demand for exhibitions, sports events and conventions.

The square roof consists of a steel framework unit, 30 feet high and 720 feet in span. It rests upon all four outer walls which take the form of trusses (60 feet in height) raised 20 feet above the ground on six tapered concrete columns. The total height of the hall from floor to ceiling is 110 feet.

The glazed walls of the ground floor are set back 30 feet. Dark grey marble, aluminium or tinted glass fill the panels so that the structure of the hall is expressed clearly both inside and outside. Mies has always built so that "the construction is the building itself".

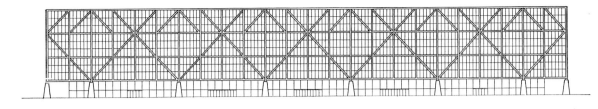

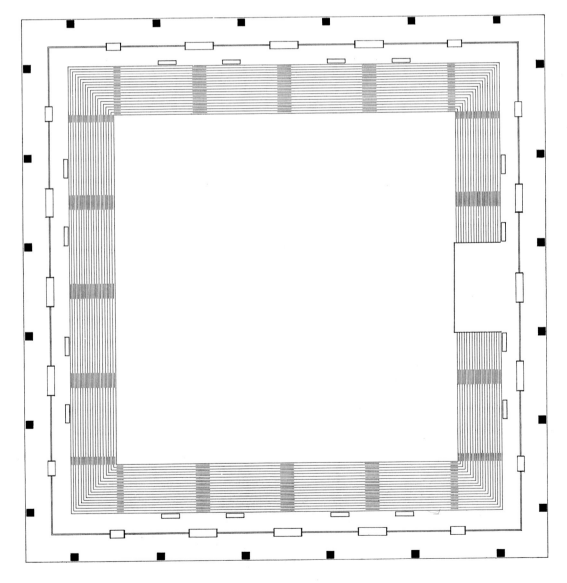

189

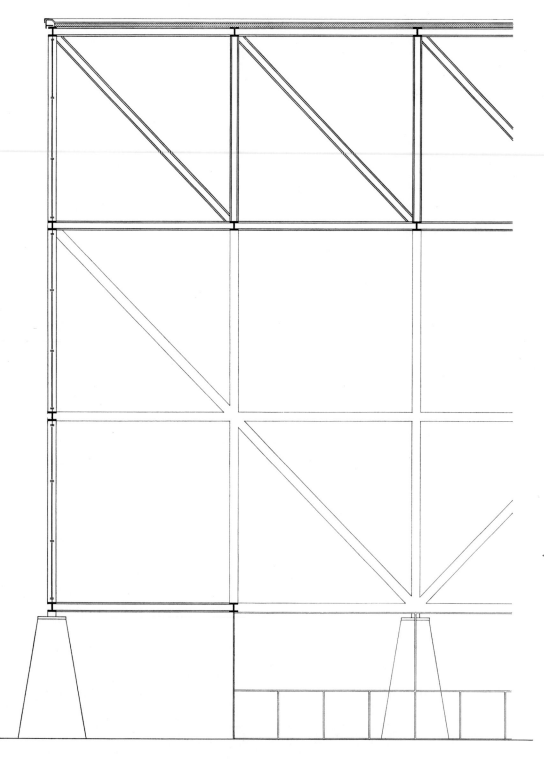

◁ Typical vertical section. Scale 1:200 (1/16″=1′ – 0″)

The roof structure is visible in the outer skin ▷

Alternative design for the outer skin. The panels ▷ ▷
are filled with uniform slabs of marble. (This model
shows the design proposed for building)

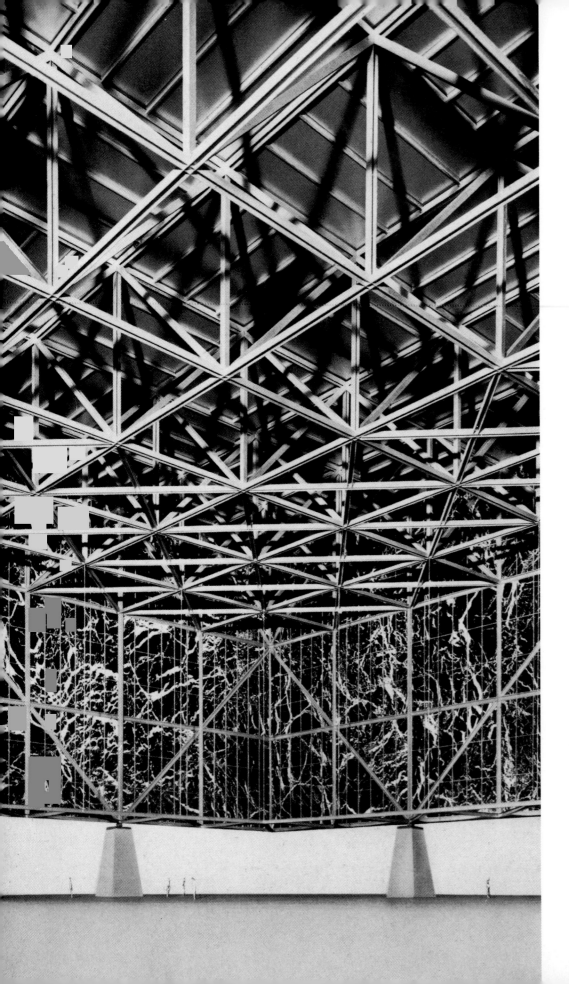

◁ Interior view of the roof structure

View of model showing outer skin ▷

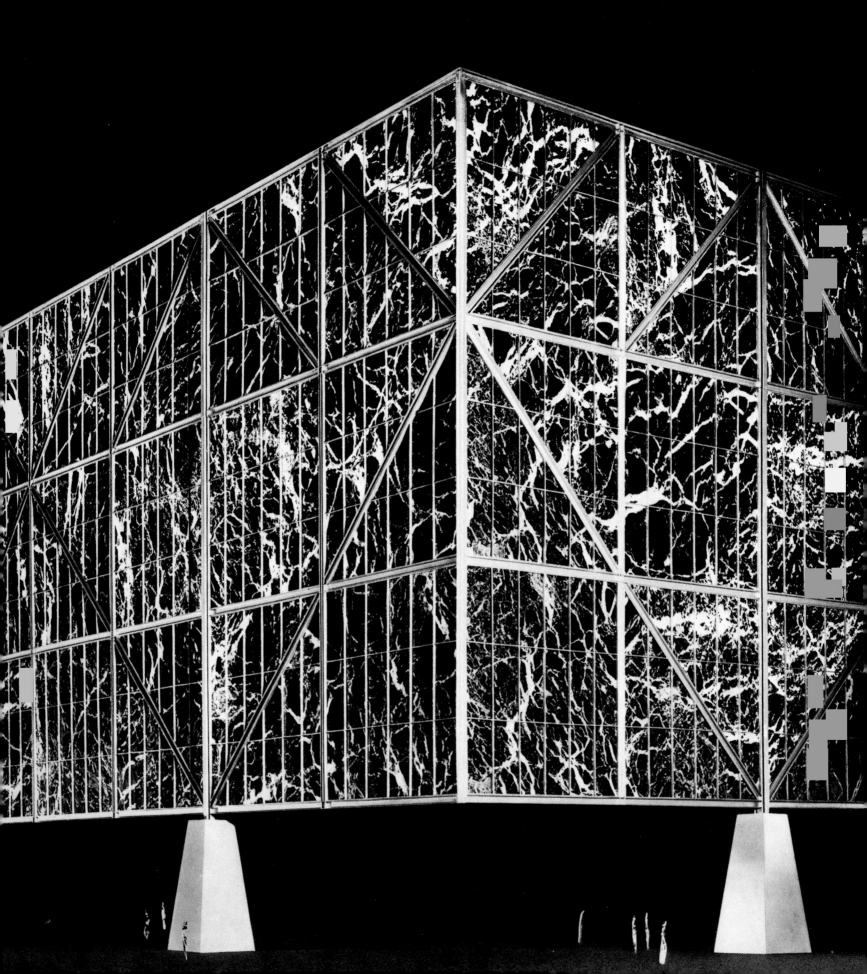

Bacardi Building, Santiago (Cuba), project 1957

The building programme called for a hall with a column-free interior which was to be built in concrete.

The roof measuring 54 × 54 metres is a rigid "egg crate" made up of intersecting concrete beams. At each of its outside edges it is supported on two concrete columns. In section the columns take the form of a cross with a "hinge" at the top to take the weight of the roof. The hall is seven metres in height and stands on a podium set in the sloping landscape. The glazed enclosing wall is set back from the roof periphery.

Prestressed concrete column cruciform in section ▷

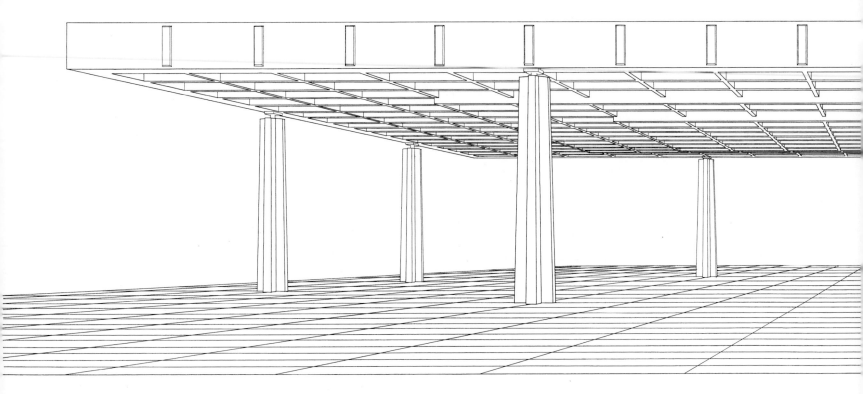

Drawing showing the "egg crate" roof and the
concrete columns

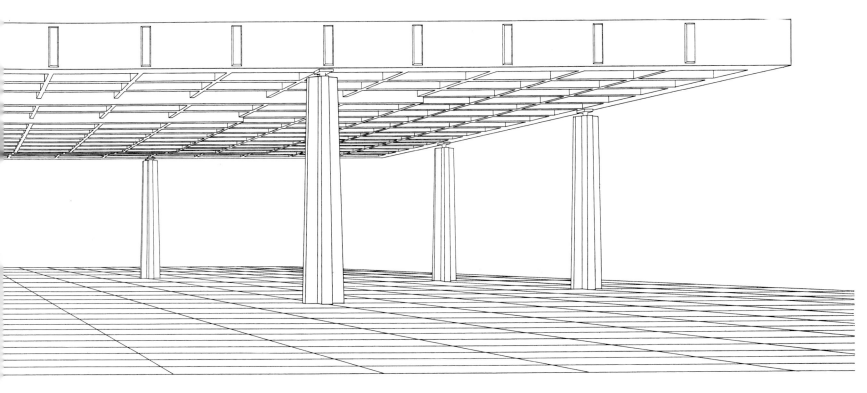

Georg-Schäfer-Museum, Schweinfurt, project 1960

The same construction scheme as for the Santiago project, but now in steel, was used for the Georg-Schäfer-Museum and the Gallery of the 20th Century. The rigid square roof plate is made of welded intersecting girders and rests upon eight steel columns of welded T-beams. There is a suspended acoustic ceiling in the large glazed hall of the museum.

A great hall can be used for a wide diversity of purposes such as an office or the exhibition of works of art. The fact that users proposed to insert a concert hall into the building on a free floor plan irrespective of the structure shows that the hall is almost infinitely flexible in the functions it can serve. In size these spacious halls are comparable to the large industrial buildings constructed by engineers: structurally they are of general validity.

Roof of steel sections supported on columns cruciform in section ▷

Gallery of the 20th Century (National Gallery), Berlin, 1962-1965

The square glass-enclosed hall for travelling art exhibitions stands on a broad terrace. Beneath the terrace is the gallery for the permanent collection, the administration and storage.

The site slopes down to its western end where the terrace forms a walled courtyard which provides daylight for the gallery rooms on the lower floor.

The roof of the hall is a flat, two-directional structure 1.80 metres deep. It consists of welded steel web-girders arranged at 3.60 metre centres in both directions and forming a square structural grid. The continuous plate is reinforced with ribs to prevent buckling. Eight steel columns, two on each side, support the roof. The roof structure measures 64.80 × 64.80 metres and the interior of the hall is 8.40 metres high.

The glazed walls are set back 7.20 metres on all sides so as to leave an arcade between the glass and the columns. The terrace and the floor of the hall are paved with granite slabs measuring 1.20 × 1.20 metres.

At the gallery level the building is a reinforced concrete structure (columns at intervals of 7.20 metres). The materials for the gallery rooms (four metres high) are plaster ceilings painted white, plywood panel walls, also painted white, and terrazzo for the floors.

The exhibition hall and museum spaces at the lower level will have an orderly arrangement of downlights for general illumination. In addition, the exhibition hall will be given a number of spotlights which can be inserted in the ceiling wherever needed. A specially designed wall-washer system will light the picture walls.

The problem of arranging works of art in spaces has always interested Mies van der Rohe. Collages of earlier buildings, for example a villa (1938) or the Museum for a Small City (1942), show how sculpture, painting and space can be integrated and indicate what the character of this museum will be.

General plan of the 20th Century Gallery.
Scale 1:800 (1/64"=1' – 0") ▷

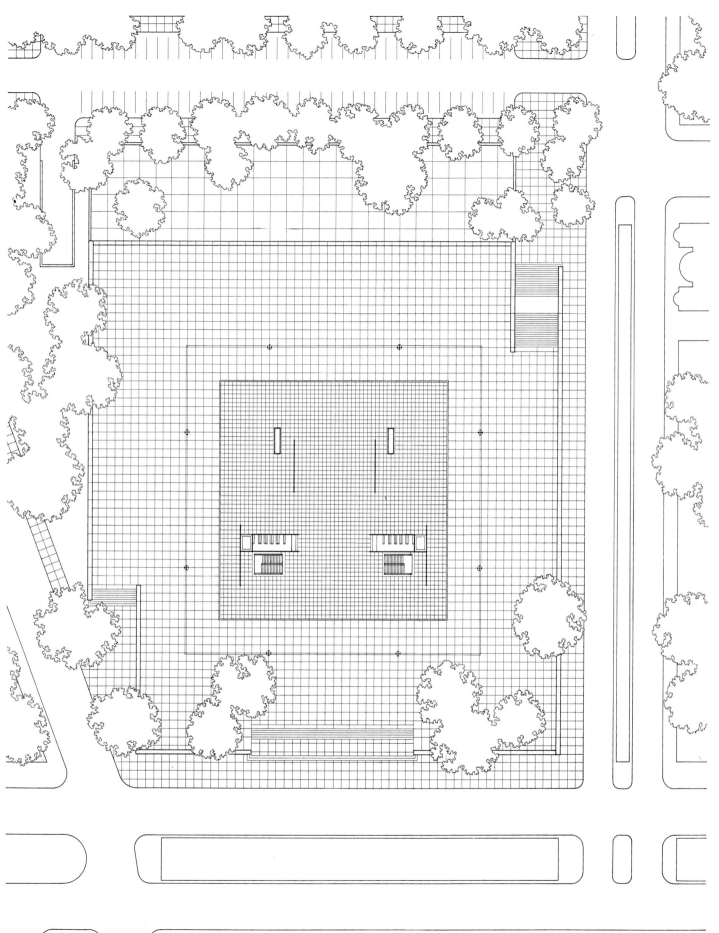

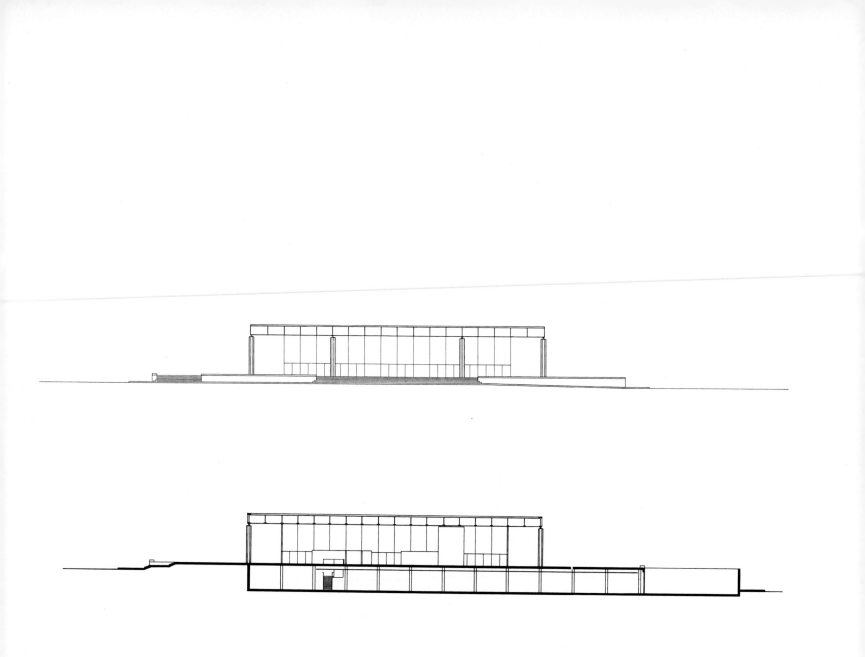

△ Front elevation and section. Scale 1:800
(1/64"=1' – 0")

In front of the terrace is a sunken portion of the   ▷
museum garden

An imposing terrace and exhibition hall are on the   ▷ ▷
same level

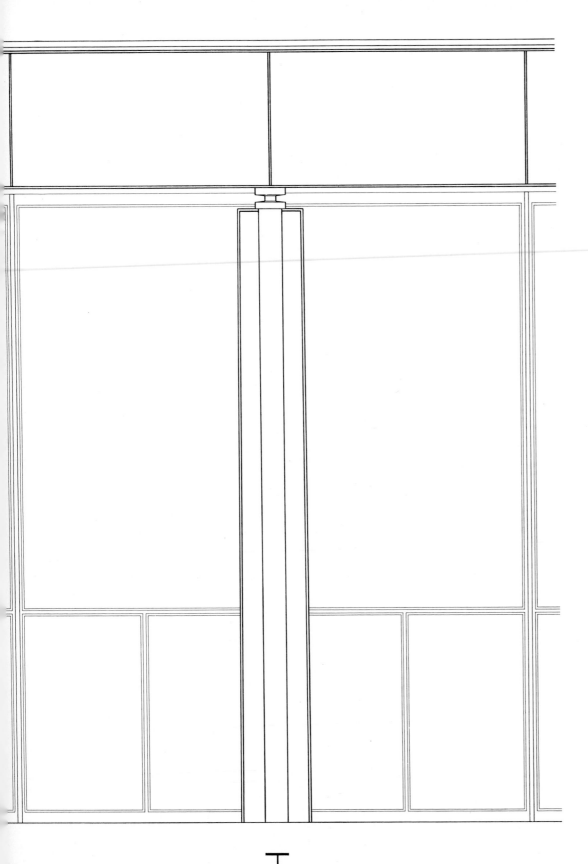

The horizontals of the roof and the verticals of the columns are clearly ordered and articulated. Elevation, scale 1:50 (1/4"=1'–0")

210

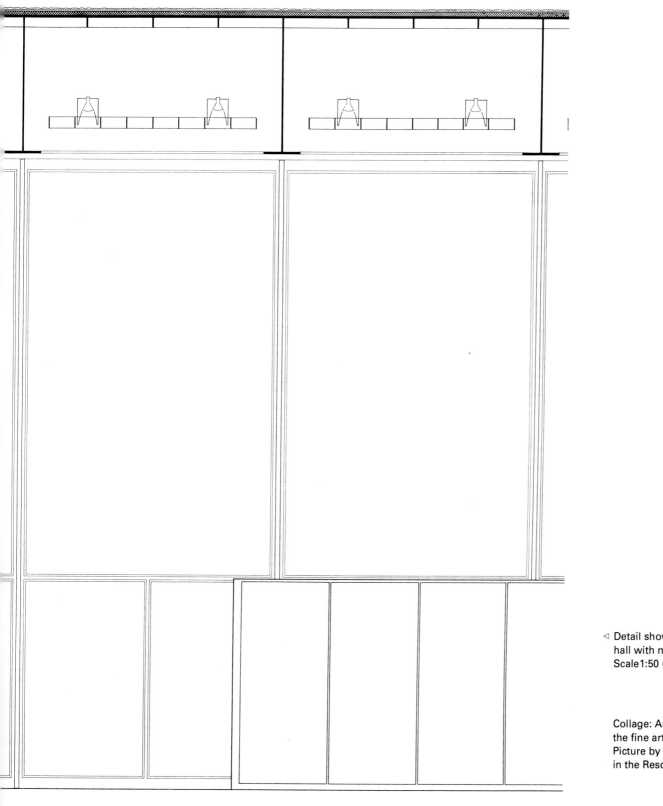

◁ Detail showing section of the exhibition
hall with movable exhibition walls.
Scale 1:50 (¼″=1′ – 0″)

Collage: Architecture combined with　▷
the fine arts.
Picture by Paul Klee "Bunte Mahlzeit"
in the Resor House (1938)

214

◁ Fountain-pen sketch: View looking through a court house (1934)

Precision in structure and the free use of a ▷ sculpture by Maillol, "L'action enchaînée" (Museum for a Small City, 1942)

Outdoor and indoor space: Water, groups of trees, ▷ ▷ sculptures and Picasso's mural "Guernica" (Museum for a Small City, 1942)

Acknowledgements

This book took shape during a number of conversations I was privileged to have with Mies van der Rohe in the impressive atmosphere of his study in Chicago in 1963 and 1964. Our aim was to set forth the essential ideas which underlie the development of the structural forms in his buildings.

There is "construction" in the very way Mies van der Rohe thinks, acts and talks. He does not design. In a slow and profound process of maturation he evolves the structure of each building, analyses it in many detailed sketches, studies each element in his mind and seeks out its potentialities and limitations until it can be fitted into the whole. Each step in the process is carried out not only in drawings but also in models. Plan and model are thus intimately related.

Mies van der Rohe attaches great importance to the workshop in his office. Here, proportion, construction and the appearance of the materials are assessed on a model. Extreme care is taken with these models: a drawing cannot give an adequate idea of the rhythm of a steel skeleton; here, the model must decide.

The examples of Mies van der Rohe's work given in this book have been arranged chronologically so as to show the development of his architecture. Illustrations and explanations are given of the basic ideas which Mies van der Rohe has pursued throughout his life, and for this reason we have confined ourselves to the most important buildings. I have taken new photographs of the buildings in America with the intention of showing their structural development. The drawings have been reduced to a uniform scale, the American in feet and the European in metres (1 metre = 39.37 inches). In the abstract collages space, work of art, material and the relationships between them are examined.

The dates in the complete list of works always indicate the year of construction and the dates in the list of contents the year in which the project commenced and the year in which the building was completed. All the texts were originally written in German. Besides a description of the buildings, which is limited to the most essential data on position, construction, material and dimensions, I have also attempted to sketch Mies van der Rohe's basic philosophy such as he passes on to his associates and pupils as a kind of education in architecture. The texts scattered throughout the book come from his diaries and our conversations.

It is a great privilege for me to express my sincerest thanks to Ludwig Mies van der Rohe for his untiring and sympathetic assistance in the preparation of this book, for his generosity in providing me with valuable original material and for the friendly atmosphere in which I worked.

The architects in his office in Chicago are associates in the best sense of the word. Never, in speaking of his works, does Mies van der Rohe use the word "I". His "we" always includes everyone working with him. I should like to thank these associates of many years' standing for their unfailing helpfulness, their advice and their corrections, more particularly Peter Carter, Dirk Lohan and Gene Summers, and John Fleming who made the ink drawings.

I should like to thank the Museum of Modern Art in New York for their courtesy in loaning drawings and collages (38, 42, 50, 54, 79, 80, 81, 214, 218), the George Danforth private collection for a charcoal sketch (16), Phyllis Lambert for a pencil sketch (152) and James Speyer for a pen sketch (216). My grateful thanks to Ogden Hannaford and Myron Goldsmith, with whom I stayed during the summer months of 1963 and 1964. The original idea of planning this book I owe to Eduard Neuenschwander and Christian Norberg Schulz. My special thanks to my friends who had a hand in the making of the book and helped me to reduce it to its essentials: Lucius Burckhardt, Antonio Hernandez, Adolf Jacob and Friedrich Störk.

I should also like to thank the Museum of Modern Art in New York for kindly placing at my disposal negatives of the earlier buildings in Germany, Hedrich Blessing for the photographs of models (89, 172, 175, 176, 195, 196, 198, 199, 205, 209, 210) and Jane Doggett and Malcolm Smith for the photograph (146). All the other photographs were provided by the publisher.

W. B., Basle, October 1964

Biography

1886	27 March, Ludwig Mies van der Rohe born in Aachen
1897–1900	Attended the Domschule at Aachen
1900–1902	Pupil at the Aachen Trade School Worked in his father's stone-mason business
1902	Trainee on building sites
1903–1904	Draughtsman working on stucco ornaments in a stucco business
1905–1907	Furniture designer with Bruno Paul in Berlin
1908–1911	Architect with Peter Behrens in Berlin
1912–1937	Own architect's practice in Berlin
1921–1925	Organizer of exhibitions for November Group
1926	In charge of the Werkbund Exhibition 'The Dwelling' Weissenhof settlement in Stuttgart
1926–1932	Vice-president of the German Werkbund
1929	Creator of the building representing Germany at the World Exhibition in Barcelona
1930–1933	Director of the Bauhaus at Dessau and Berlin
1931	Head of the Werkbund section 'The Dwelling of Our Time' at the Berlin Building Exhibition
1938	Emigrated to the USA
1938–1958	Director of the School of Architecture of the Illinois Institute of Technology (IIT), Chicago Replanning of campus
1938	Own architect's practice in Chicago
1948	First curtain wall of steel and glass in the apartment towers in Chicago
1950	Development of column-free interiors in hall constructions with wide-span roofs
1959	Member of the Order Pour le Mérite (Federal Republic of Germany) Distinctions and honours in Europe and USA
1963	Presidential Medal of Freedom, conferred by the President of the United States
1969	17 August, Mies van der Rohe died in Chicago

Buildings and projects by Mies van der Rohe

1907	Riehl House, Berlin-Neubabelsberg, Germany
1911	Perls House, Berlin-Zehlendorf, Germany (later Fuchs House)
1912	Project: Kröller House, The Hague, The Netherlands Project: Bismarck Monument, Bingen, Germany
1913	House on the Heerstrasse, Berlin, Germany
1914	Urbig House, Berlin-Neubabelsberg, Germany Project: House for the Architect, Werder, Germany (two versions)
1919	Project: Kempner House, Berlin, Germany
1919–1921	Project: Glass Skyscraper
1921	Kempner House, Berlin, Germany (destroyed) Project: Office Building, Friedrichstrasse, Berlin, Germany Project: Petermann House, Berlin-Neubabelsberg, Germany
1922	Project: Concrete Office Building, Berlin, Germany Project: Concrete Country House Project: Lessing House, Berlin-Neubabelsberg, Germany Project: Eliat House, Nedlitz, near Potsdam, Germany
1923	Project: Brick Country House
1924	Mosler House, Berlin-Neubabelsberg, Germany Project: Traffic Tower, Berlin, Germany
1925–1926	Wolf House, Guben, Germany
1926	Monument to Karl Liebknecht and Rosa Luxemburg, Berlin, Germany (destroyed)
1926–1927	Municipal Housing Development, Afrikanische Strasse, Berlin, Germany
1927	Werkbund Exhibition, Weissenhofsiedlung, Stuttgart, Germany Apartment Building, Weissenhofsiedlung, Stuttgart, Germany Silk Exhibit, Exposition de la Mode, Berlin, Germany (with Lilly Reich)
1928	Addition to Fuchs House (Perls House), Berlin-Zehlendorf, Germany Hermann Lange House, Krefeld, Germany Esters House, Krefeld, Germany Project: Remodelling of Alexanderplatz, Berlin, Germany Project: Adam Building, Leipzigerstrasse, Berlin, Germany Project: Bank Building, Stuttgart, Germany
1928–1929	German Pavilion, International Exhibition, Barcelona, Spain (demolished), reconstructed 1986 Electricity Pavilion, International Exhibition, Barcelona, Spain (demolished) Industrial Exhibits, International Exhibition, Barcelona, Spain (with Lilly Reich)
1928–1930	Tugendhat House, Brno, Czechoslovakia (badly damaged)

1929	Project: Office Building, Friedrichstrasse, Berlin, Germany (second scheme)
1930	Apartment Interior, New York, N.Y. Project: Country Club, Krefeld, Germany Project: War Memorial, Berlin, Germany Project: Gericke House, Wannsee, Berlin, Germany
1931	House, Berlin Building Exhibition, Berlin, Germany (demolished) Apartment for a Bachelor, Berlin Building Exhibition, Berlin, Germany (demolished)
1931	Projects: Court Houses
1932	Lemcke House, Berlin, Germany
1933	Factory Building and Power House for the Silk Industry, Vereinigte Seidenwebereien AG, Krefeld, Germany Project: Reichsbank, Berlin, Germany
1934	Mining Exhibits, Deutsches Volk, Deutsche Arbeit, Exhibition, Berlin, Germany Project: House for the Architect, Tyrol, Austria Project: German Pavilion, International Exhibition, Brussels, Belgium Project: Service Station
1935	Project: Ulrich Lange House, Krefeld, Germany Project: Hubbe House, Magdeburg, Germany
1937	Project: Administration Building for the Silk Industry, Vereinigte Seidenwebereien AG, Krefeld, Germany
1938	Project: Resor House, Jackson Hole, Wyoming
1939	Preliminary Campus Plan, Illinois Institute of Technology, Chicago, Illinois
1940–1941	Master Plan, Illinois Institute of Technology, Chicago, Illinois
1942	Project: Museum for a Small City
1943	Project: Concert Hall
1942–1943	Metals Research Building for Armour Research Foundation, Illinois Institute of Technology Research Institute, Chicago, Illinois (Associate Architects: Holabird and Root)
1944	Project: Library and Administration Building, Illinois Institute of Technology, Chicago, Illinois
1944–1946	Engineering Research Building for Armour Research Foundation, Illinois Institute of Technology Research Institute, Chicago, Illinois (Associate Architects: Holabird and Root)

1945	Studies for Classroom Buildings, Illinois Institute of Technology, Chicago, Illinois Project: Mooringsport Power Station, Mooringsport, Louisiana Meredosia Power Station, Meredosia, Louisiana Havana Power Station, Havana, Illinois (with Sargent and Lundy, Engineers)
1945–1946	Alumni Memorial Hall, Illinois Institute of Technology, Chicago, Illinois (Associate Architects: Holabird and Root) Perlstein Hall (Metallurgical and Chemical Engineering Building), Illinois Institute of Technology, Chicago, Illinois (Associate Architects: Holabird and Root) Wishnick Hall (Chemistry Building), Illinois Institute of Technology, Chicago, Illinois (Associate Architects: Friedman, Alschuler and Sincere) Project: Cantor Drive-in Restaurant, Indianapolis, Indiana
1945–1950	Fox River House (Farnsworth House), Plano, Illinois Boiler Plant, Illinois Institute of Technology, Chicago, Illinois
1946–1947	Project: Cantor House, Indianapolis, Indiana
1946–1949	Promontory Apartments, Indianapolis, Indiana (Associate Architects: Pace Associates, and Holsman, Holsman, Klekamp and Taylor)
1947	Central Vault, Illinois Institute of Technology, Chicago, Illinois Project: Theatre Project: Gymnasium and Swimming-pool, Illinois Institute of Technology, Chicago, Illinois
1947–1950	Institute of Gas Technology, Illinois Institute of Technology, Chicago, Illinois (Associate Architects: Friedman, Alschuler and Sincere)
1948	Project: Student Union Building, Illinois Institute of Technology, Chicago, Illinois
1948–1950	Association of American Railroads Administration Building, Illinois Institute of Technology, Chicago, Illinois (Associate Architects: Friedman, Alschuler and Sincere)
1948–1951	860–880 Lake Shore Drive Apartments, Chicago, Illinois (Associate Architects: Pace Associates, and Holsman, Holsman, Klekamp and Taylor) Interior, The Arts Club of Chicago, Chicago, Illinois Project: Algonquin Apartments, Chicago, Illinois (two versions)
1948–1953	Mechanical Engineering Building for the Association of American Railroads, Illinois Institute of Technology, Chicago, Illinois (Associate Architects: Friedman, Alschuler and Sincere)
1949–1950	Project: Cantor Commercial Center Office Building, Indianapolis, Indiana
1949–1952	Chapel, Illinois Institute of Technology, Chicago, Illinois
1950	Project: Caine House, Winnetka, Illinois Project: Dormitory and Fraternity House, Illinois Institute of Technology, Chicago, Illinois
1950–1956	Crown Hall (Architecture, City Planning and Design Building), Illinois Institute of Technology, Chicago, Illinois (Associate Architects: Pace Associates)
1950–1951	Project: Steel Frame Prefabricated Row House Project: Fifty Foot by Fifty Foot House
1950–1952	Mechanical Engineering Research Building I, Illinois Institute of Technology Research Institute, Chicago, Illinois (Associate Architects: Friedman, Alschuler and Sincere) Project: Berke Office Building, Indianapolis, Indiana
1951–1952	McCormick House, Elmhurst, Illinois Project: Pi Lamda Phi Fraternity House, Bloomington, Indiana
1951–1953	Carman Hall, Illinois Institute of Technology, Chicago, Illinois (Associate Architects: Pace Associates)
1952–1953	Commons Building, Illinois Institute of Technology, Chicago, Illinois (Associate Architects: Friedman, Alschuler and Sincere) Project: National Theatre, Mannheim, Germany
1952–1955	Cunningham Hall, Illinois Institute of Technology, Chicago, Illinois (Associate Architects: Pace Associates)
1953–1954	Project: Convention Hall, Chicago, Illinois
1953–1956	Commonwealth Promenade Apartments, Chicago, Illinois (Associate Architects: Friedman, Alschuler and Sincere) 900 Esplanade Apartments, Chicago, Illinois (Associate Architects: Friedman, Alschuler and Sincere)
1954	Master Plan for the Museum of Fine Arts, Houston, Texas
1954–1958	Seagram Building, 375 Park Avenue, New York (in association with Philip Johnson; Associate Architects: Kahn and Jacobs) Cullinan Hall, The Museum of Fine Arts, Houston, Texas (Associate Architects: Staub, Rather and Howze)
1955	Project: Lubin Apartment Hotel, New York, N. Y.
1955–1956	Master Plan for Lafayette Park, Housing Project, Detroit, Michigan
1955–1957	Association of American Railroads Laboratory Building, Illinois Institute of Technology, Chicago, Illinois (Associate Architects: Friedman, Alschuler and Sincere) Physics-Electronics Research Building, Illinois Institute of Technology Research Institute, Chicago, Illinois (Associate Architects: Naess & Murphy)
1956–1958	Metals Research Building, Illinois Institute of Technology Research Institute, Chicago, Illinois (Associate Architects: Holabird and Root)
1957	Project: United States Consulate, São Paulo, Brazil Project: Quadrangles Apartments, Brooklyn, New York Project: Quadrangles Apartments, Brooklyn, New York Project: Bacardi Office Building, Santiago de Cuba, Cuba Project: Kaiser Office Building, Chicago, Illinois Project: Commercial Building, Pratt Institute, Brooklyn, New York
1957–1958	Project: Battery Park Apartment Development, New York, N. Y.

1957–1961	Bacardi Office Building, Mexico City, Mexico (Associate Architects: Saenz-Cancio-Martin-Gutierrez)
1958	Pavilion Apartments, Lafayette Park, Detroit, Michigan Town Houses, Lafayette Park, Detroit, Michigan
1958–1959	Project: Seagram Office Building, Chicago, Illinois
1958–1960	Pavilion Apartments and Colonnade Apartments, Colonnade Park, Newark, New Jersey
1959	Project: Mies van der Rohe Exhibition for V Bienal Exhibit, São Paulo, Brazil
1959–1963	Project: Friedrich Krupp Administration Building, Essen, Germany
1959–1964	Chicago Federal Center, U. S. Courthouse and Federal Office and U. S. Post Office Building (Joint Venture: Schmidt, Garden & Erikson, Mies van der Rohe, C. F. Murphy Associates, and A. Epstein & Sons, Inc.)
1960–1961	Project: Schäfer Museum, Schweinfurt, Germany
1960–1963	Home Federal Savings and Loan Association of Des Moines, Des Moines, Iowa (Associate Architects: Smith-Vorhees-Jenson) One Charles Center, Office Building, Baltimore, Maryland 2400 Lakeview Apartment Building, Chicago, Illinois (Associate Architects: Greenberg and Finfer)
1961	Project: Mountain Place, Montreal, Quebec
1962–1965	Social Service Administration Building, The University of Chicago, Chicago, Illinois Meredith Memorial Hall, Drake University, Des Moines, Iowa
1962–1968	New National Gallery, West Berlin, Germany The Science Center, Duquesne University, Pittsburgh, Pennsylvania
1963	Lafayette Towers, Lafayette Park, Detroit, Michigan
1963–1965	Highfield House, Apartment Building, Baltimore, Maryland
1963–1969	Toronto-Dominion Centre, Toronto, Ontario (Architects: John B. Parkin Associates and Bregman and Hamann; Consulting Architect: Mies van der Rohe)
1965–1968	Westmount Square, Montreal, Quebec (Resident Architects: Greenspoon, Freedlander, Plachta & Kryton)
1966	Project: Church Street South K-4 School, New Haven, Connecticut Project: Foster City, Apartment Buildings, San Mateo, California District of Columbia Public Library, Washington, D. C.
1966–1969	Project: Houston Museum Addition, Houston, Texas
1967	Mansion House Square Project, London, England (in association with William Holford and Partners) I. B. M. Regional Office Building, Chicago, Illinois (Joint Venture with C. F. Murphy Associates)
1967–1968	Esso Service Station, Nuns Island, Montreal, Quebec (Resident Architect: Paul LaPointe)
1967–1969	High-Rise Apartment Building No.1, Nuns Island, Montreal, Quebec (Resident Architect: Philip Bobrow) Project: King Broadcasting Studios, Seattle, Washington
1967–1970	111 East Wacker Drive, Illinois Central Air Rights Development, Chicago, Illinois
1968	Project: Commerzbank AG, Office Building and Bank, Frankfurt/Main, Germany
1968–1969	High-Rise Apartment Buildings No. 2 and 3, Nuns Island, Montreal, Quebec (Resident Architect: Edgar Tornay) Project: Northwest Plaza Project, Chicago, Illinois Project: Dominion Square Project, Montreal, Quebec

Bibliography

Bill, Max
Ludwig Mies van der Rohe. Il Balcone, Milano 1955.

Blake, Peter
Mies van der Rohe – Architecture and Structure. Pelican Books, Baltimore 1960.

Blaser, Werner, und Burckhardt, Lucius
Objektive Architektur – Mies van der Rohe, Werk. Bern, November 1964.

Blaser, Werner
Mies van der Rohe – Die Kunst der Struktur. Verlag für Architektur, Zürich 1965.
Mies van der Rohe. Praeger Publishers, New York 1972, and A. D. A. Edita, Tokyo 1976.
Il design di Mies van der Rohe. Electa Editrice, Milano 1980.
Continuing the Chicago School of Architecture. Birkhäuser Verlag, Basel 1981.

Bonta, János P.
Mies van der Rohe. Barcelona 1929, Editional Gustavo Gili S. A., Barcelona 1976.
Ludwig Mies van der Rohe. Henschelverlag Kunst und Gesellschaft, Berlin 1983.

Carter, Peter
Mies van der Rohe, Architectural Design. London, March 1961.
Mies van der Rohe at Work. Phaidon Press Limited Publishers, London 1974.

Condit, Carl W.
The Chicago School of Architecture 1875–1925. The University of Chicago Press, 1963.

Drexler, Arthur
Ludwig Mies van der Rohe. George Braziller Inc., New York 1960.
Mies van der Rohe Centennial. The Museum of Modern Art, New York 1986.

Dunster, David
Houses 1900–1944. Rizzoli, New York 1985.

Glaeser, Ludwig
Ludwig Mies van der Rohe. The Museum of Modern Art, New York 1969.

Grube, Oswald W.
100 Jahre Architektur in Chicago. Die Neue Sammlung, München 1973.

Grube, Oswald W., Pran, Peter C., and Schulze, Franz
100 Years of Architecture in Chicago. Museum of Contemporary Art, Chicago 1976.

Hilberseimer, Ludwig
Mies van der Rohe. Paul Theobald Publisher, Chicago 1956.
Die Entfaltung einer Planungsidee. Verlag Ullstein, Berlin 1963.

Illinois Institute of Technology
Mies van der Rohe, Architect as Educator. Chicago 1986.

Joedecke, Jürgen
Die Weißenhofsiedlung. Karl Krämer Verlag, Stuttgart 1968.

Johnson, Philip C.
Mies van der Rohe. The Museum of Modern Art, New York 1947, and Verlag Gert Hatje, Stuttgart 1956.

Persitz, Alexander
L'œuvre de Mies van der Rohe. L'Architecture d'aujourd'hui, Paris, septembre 1958.

Schulze, Franz
Mies van der Rohe, Interior Space. The Art Club of Chicago, 1982.

Spaeth, David
Mies van der Rohe – Bibliography. Garland Publishing Inc., New York 1980.
Mies van der Rohe. Rizzoli, New York 1985.

Speyer, James
Ludwig Mies van der Rohe. The Art Institute of Chicago, 1968, and Akademie der Künste, Berlin. 1968.

Tegethoff, Wolf
Mies van der Rohe, Die Villen und Landhausprojekte. Verlag Richard Bacht, Essen 1981.

Wingler, Hans M.
Das Bauhaus 1919–1933. M. DuMont Schauberg, Köln 1968.
Kleine Bauhaus-Fibel. Bauhaus-Archiv-Verlag, Berlin 1974.

Württembergischer Kunstverein
50 Jahre Bauhaus, 1968, and Supplement 1969, Stuttgart.

After Mies or: thirty years later

Thirty years have elapsed since I worked on this book, "The Art of Structure", with Mies van der Rohe in Chicago. Mies died there on 17 August 1969 at the age of 83 years. He lies buried in Graceland Cemetery under a simple slab of stone, not far from the monumental tomb of Louis Sullivan. His works in the Museum of Modern Art bear the label: "American architect German born".

The last three decades of Mies van der Rohe's life and work witnessed the appearance in Chicago of his steel-and-glass architecture. Rightly or wrongly, Business made this architecture its prerogative and, even after Mies' death, it received worldwide acclaim and found many imitators. Unfortunately this often led to Mies being misunderstood, for no one can imitate him. What imitators should have done, of course, was to adopt his principles as the basis for their own work and thus take his architecture a step forward.

Over the intervening period of thirty years it is possible to see this book in retrospect: in spite of the plethora of publications appearing on Mies van der Rohe, he still remains a challenge. It is for this reason that this standard work, which has long been out of print but bears the stamp of his personal authorization, is being brought out in a new and unaltered edition. Through Mies, with his blend of western thought and eastern wisdom, I learned how to recognize the inner laws by which architecture evolves. The influence his exceptional artistic intelligence had on architecture is still in evidence everywhere – in spite of every post-modern attempt to repudiate him.

For Mies van der Rohe a building was an immediately intelligible structuring work of art which embodied timeless messages. From the very outset he argued for the dissolution of rigid forms into transparent functions. Solid masonry was replaced by light walls of glass: inside is outside … outside is inside. Layer by layer he erected his buildings like a craftsman obsessed with precision. It is a common saying with us that the "devil is in the details" but in the Miesean case it is rather God himself. The self-given nature of his buildings stems from his creation of form through the senses and the intellectuality of his concentration. His work was rather a felt awareness, a calm state of knowledge which had little need of words.

To build is to think, to find ideas worthy of consideration. In Mies' work we find a multiplicity of such qualities, and these continue to elicit new questions and foster new experience. This new edition will therefore fulfil its purpose only if, on the basis of Mies' concepts and solutions, it prompts further reappraisal. Something Mies said runs like a thread through the book and explains why he is once more of current significance. "I feel," Mies once said, "that the influence my works have on other people rests on their rationality. Everyone can work on it without becoming an imitator. Because it is absolutely objective. I believe that if I myself found something objective, I would make use of it. Who it comes from is a matter of no importance."

Some books from Mies' library

The complete contents of Mies' personal library have been excellently catalogued by Richard Seidel. These books are in the custody of the Department of Special Collections, the Library, University of Illinois at Chicago Circle. In 1975, at my request, members of Mies' family, and a close friend (with whom he often read) identified the following titles as the ones most important to Mies. In 1952, Mies told students at the School of Design of the North Carolina State College that he owned 3,000 books in Germany and that he had brought 300 with him to America. Of these he could have sent back 270. He would not, he said, have discovered the remaining thirty unless he had read the 3,000 books. It is in this light that this list of some of his books (collection in the possession of the family) should be considered.

Adler, Mortimer J.
The Difference of Man and the Difference It Makes.
Holt, Rinehart and Winston, 1967.

Aquinas, Thomas
The Basic Writings of Thomas Aquinas. Edited by Anton C. Pegis. Random House, New York 1945.

Ardrey, Robert
The Territorial Imperative. Atheneum, New York 1966.
African Genesis. Dell, New York 1961.

Aristoteles
Über die Seele. Übertragen von Adolf Lasson. Eugen Diederichs, Jena 1924.

Aristotle
The Student's Oxford Aristotle, Politics and Poetics. Oxford University Press, 1942

Berlage. H. P.
Studies over Bouwkunst, Styl en Samenleving. W.L. and J. Brusse le Rotterdam, 1910.
Grundlagen und Entwicklung der Architektur. W. L. and J. Brusse, n. d.

Bieber, Margarete
The Greek and Roman Theater. Princeton University Press, 1961.

Blaser, Werner
Tempel und Teehaus in Japan. Otto Walter Verlag, Olten 1955.

Boeke, Kees
Cosmic View. The Universe in 40 Jumps. J. Day, New York 1957.

Boetticher, Karl
Die Tektonik der Hellenen. F. Riegel, Potsdam 1852.

Bohr, Niels
Atomic Physics and Human Knowledge. John Wiley & Sons, New York 1958.

Bronowski, J.
Science and Human Values. Julian Messner, New York 1956.

Burger, Fritz
Die Villen des Palladio. Bayrische Akademie der Wissenschaften. Herausgegeben von Klinkhardt & Biermann, Leipzig 1909.

Buytendijk, F. J. J.
Erziehung zur Demut. A. Henn Verlag, Ratingen 1962.

Cali, François
Das Gesetz der Gotik. Prestel Verlag, München 1963.
L'Ordre grec, essai sur le temple dorique. Photographies de Serge Moulnier, Arthaud, Paris 1958.
Architecture of truth. G. Braziller, New York 1957.

Chamberlain, Houston Stewart 1855–1927
Die Grundlagen des neunzehnten Jahrhunderts (2 Bde.). F. Bruckmann, München 1909.

Condit, Carl W.
The Rise of the Skyscraper. The University of Chicago Press, 1952.

Cornford, F.M.
Principium Sapientiae, The Origins of Greek Philosophical Thought. Cambridge University Press, 1952.
The Unwritten Philosophy and Other Essays. Cambridge University Press, 1950.

Dessauer, Friedrich
Philosophie der Technik. Friedrich Cohen, Bonn 1927.

Dornbusch, Charles
Pennsylvania German Barns. Schlechter's, Allentown, Pennsylvania 1958.

Dreuermann, Fritz
Naturerkenntnis. Band 6 von Das Weltbild, herausgegeben von Hans Prinzhorn. Müller & Kiepenheuer Verlag, Potsdam 1928.

Durm, Josef
Die Baukunst der Griechen. Alfred Kroner Verlag, 1910.

Eddington, A. S.
Die Naturwissenschaft auf neuen Bahnen. Friedrich Viehweg, Braunschweig 1935.
The Expanding Universe. Ann Arbor Paperbacks, 1958.

Egdell, G. H.
The American Architecture of Today. Charles Scribner's Sons, 1928.

Einstein, Albert
Ideas and Opinions. Crown, New York 1954.
Out of My Later Years. Philosophical Library, New York 1950.

Eiseley, Loren .
(the anthropologist and historian of the University of Pennsylvania)
The Mind as Nature. Harper & Row, New York 1962. (The John Dewey Society Lectureship, 5.)

The Immense Journey. Random House, New York 1957.
Darwin's Century. Doubleday, New York 1968.
The Firmament of Time. Atheneum, New York 1966.
Francis Bacon and the Modern Dilemma. University of Nebraska Press, Lincoln, Neb. 1962.

Eucken, Rudolph
Die Lebensanschauungen der grossen Denker. Leipzig 1912.

Fischer, Theodor
Zwei Vorträge über Proportionen. Oldenburg Verlag, 1934.

Fitchem, John
The Construction of Gothic Cathedrals. Oxford at the Clarendon Press, 1961.

Francé, Raoul F.
Der Weg zu mir. Alfred Kroner-Verlag, Leipzig 1927.
Streifzüge im Wassertropfen. Kosmos-Verlag, Stuttgart 1906.

Freyer, Hans
Theorie des gegenwärtigen Zeitalters. Deutsche Verlagsanstalt, Stuttgart 1958.

Fuchs, Eduard
Illustrierte Sittengeschichte (3 Bde., Ergänzungsbände). Verlag Albert Langen, München 1912 (Privatdruck).

Gebser, Hans
Abendländische Wandlung. Ullstein, Frankfurt a. M. 1960.

Ghiselin, Brewster
The Creative Process. A Mentor Book. 1952.

Gilson, Etienne
Being and Some Philosophers. Pontifical Institute of Medieval Studies, Toronto 1949.

Gleichen-Russwurm, A. von
Die gotische Welt. Verlag Julius Hoffmann, 1919.

Goodyear, William Henry
Greek Refinements, Studies in Temperamental Architecture. The Yale University Press, 1912.

Gotshalk, D. W
Art and the Social Order. University of Chicago Press, 1947.

Grohmann, Will
Paul Klee. W. Kohlhammer, Stuttgart 1954.

Guardini, Romano
Über das Wesen des Kunstwerkes. Rainer Wunderlich-Verlag, Tübingen 1959.

Hartmann, Nicolai
Das Problem des geistigen Seins. Verlag Walter Gruyter & Co., Berlin 1933.

Heidegger, Martin
Kant und das Problem der Metaphysik. Verlag Diederich Cohen, Bonn 1929.

Hertz, Richard
Man on a Rock. Chapel Hill, The University of North Carolina Press, 1946.

Hitchcock and Johnson
The International Style: Architecture Since 1922. W. W. Norton & Company, 1932.

Hoffer, Eric
The True Believer. New American Library, New York 1963.
The Temper of Our Times. Harper & Row, New York 1967.

Hoyle, Fred
The Nature of the Universe. Harper & Brothers, New York 1950.

Hutchins, Robert M.
The University of Utopia. The University of Chicago Press, 1953.

Huxley, Aldous
Ends and Means. Harper & Brothers, 1937.

Huxley, Julian
Evolution, The Modern Synthesis. Harper & Brothers, New York 1942.
New Bottles for New Wine. Harper, New York 1957.

Jaeger, Werner
Paideia: The Ideals of Greek Culture. Volume 1: Archaic Greece. The Mind of
Athens. Oxford University Press, 1945.

Jefferson, Thomas
Life and Selected Writings of Thomas Jefferson. Edited by Adrienne Koch and
William Peden. The Modern Library, 1944.

Kahler, Heinz
Wandlungen der antiken Form. Münchner Verlag, 1949.

Kant, Immanuel
Kritik der reinen Vernunft. Insel Verlag, 1922.

Kapp, Reginald O.
Towards a Unified Cosmology. Basic Books, New York 1960.

Kerler, Dietrich Heinrich
Weltwille und Wertwille. Alfred Kroner Verlag, 1925.

Kiesler, Frederick
Inside the Endless House. Simon and Schuster, 1964.

Klopher, Paul
Von Palladio bis Schinkel. Paul Neff Verlag, 1911.

Konfuzius
Gespräche. Diederichs, Jena 1921.

Le Corbusier
Aircraft. The Studio Publications Inc., 1935.

Lerner, Max
The Age of Overkill. Simon and Schuster, New York 1962.

Lorenz, Konrad
On Aggression. Harcourt, Brace-World, New York 1966.

Lowe, Victor, Hartshorne, Charles and Johnson, A. H.
Whitehead and The Modern World. Beacon Press, Boston 1950.

Mann, Thomas
Last Essays. Alfred A. Knopf, New York 1959.

Maritain, Jacques
The Range of Reason. Charles Scribner's Sons, New York 1953.
The Rights of Man and Natural Law. Charles Scribner's Sons, 1943.
Philosophy of Nature. Philosophical Library, New York 1951.
An Introduction to Philosophy. Sheed & Ward, Inc. n.d.

Mossel, Ernst
Vom Geheimnis der Form und der Urform des Seins. Deutsche Verlagsanstalt, 1938.

Munitz, Milton K.
Theories of the Universe. The Free Press, Glencoe, Illinois 1957.

Nef, John
Bridges of Human Understanding. University Publishers, New York 1964.
A Search for Civilization. Regnery, 1962.
The United States and Civilization. The University of Chicago Press, 1942.

Novalis
The Novices of Sais. Illustrations with 60 drawings by Paul Klee. C. Valentin,
New York 1949.

Oparin, A. I.
The Origin of Life. Dover Publications, New York 1938 (1953)

Oppenheimer, F. Robert
The Open Mind. Eight Lectures (and others). Simon & Schuster, New York
1955.

Ortega y Gasset, Jose (1883–1955)
The Origin of Philosophy. W. W. Norton, New York 1967.
What is Philosophy? W. W. Norton, New York 1960.
On Love. World Publishing Co., Cleveland 1963.
The Dehumanization of Art (other writings on art and culture). Doubleday,
Garden City N.Y. 1956.
Invertebrate Spain. W. W. Norton, New York 1937.
History as a System. W. W. Norton, New York 1961.
The Modern Theme. Harper & Brothers, New York 1961.
Man & People. W. W. Norton, New York 1957.
Man and Crisis. W. W. Norton, New York 1962.

Panofsky, Erwin
Gothic Architecture and Scholasticism. The Archabbey Press, 1951.

Prevost, Jean
Eiffel. Les Editions Rieder, 1929.

Price, Lucien
Dialogues of Alfred North Whitehead. An Atlantic Monthly Press Book, Little
Brown and Company, Boston 1954.

Riehl, Alois
Philosophie der Gegenwart. Leipzig, 1908.

Rodin, Auguste
Cathedrals of France. Beacon Press, 1965 (original publication, 1914).

Rourke, Constance
The Roots of American Culture. Harcourt, Brace & Company, New York 1942.

Runes, Dagobert D.
The Dictionary of Philosophy. Philosophical Library, New York 1942.

Russell, Bertrand
Authority and the Individual. Beacon Press, Boston 1949.
Bertrand Russell's Best. Selected by Robert Egner. Mentor Book, 1958.
The Scientific Outlook. The Norton Library, 1931 (1959).

Scheler, Max
Die Wissensformen und die Gesellschaft, Problem einer Soziologie des Wissens. Der Neue Geistes-Verlag, Leipzig 1926.

Schneer, Cecil J.
The Search for Order. Harper & Brothers, 1960.

Schopenhauer, Arthur
Sämtliche Werke in fünf Bänden. Insel Verlag. n. d.

Schrödinger, Erwin
What is Life? And Other Scientific Essays. Doubleday, Garden City. N.Y. 1956.
Was ist Leben? Die lebende Zelle mit den Augen eines Physikers betrachtet. L. Lehne-Verlag, München 1951.
Nature of the Greeks. Cambridge University Press, 1954.
Mind and Matter. Cambridge University Press, 1958.
My View of the World. The University Press, Cambridge 1964.
Science and Humanism, Physics in Our Time. Cambridge University Press, 1952.

Schwarz, Rudolf
The Church Incarnate, The Sacred Function of Christian Architecture. Henry Regnery Co., Chicago 1958 (Mies helped very much with the translation – that is, he helped Cynthia Harris to understand Schwarz's ideas).
Von der Bebauung der Erde. Verlag Lambert Schneider, Heidelberg 1949.
Vom Bau der Kirche. Heidelberg 1947.
Wegweisung der Technik. Aachener Werkbücher, Band 1.

Semper, Gottfried
Der Stil (2 Bde.). Friedrich Bruckmann's Verlag, München 1878.

Shapley, Harlow
Of Stars and Men, The Human Response to an Expanding Universe. Beacon Press, Boston 1958.

Smith, Huston
The Religions of Man. Harper & Row, New York 1958.

Stahl, Fritz (pseud.) Karl Friedrich Schinkel
Schinkel-Monographie. E. Wasmuth, Berlin 1912.

Sullivan, Louis H.
The Autobiography of an Idea. Press of the A. I. A., New York 1924.

Sun Tzu
The Art of War. Translated by Samuel B. Griffith. Oxford at the Clarendon Press, 1963.

St. Augustine
The City of God. London: J. M. Dent & Sons Ltd., New York (first published edition E. P. Dutton & Co. Ltd., 1931).

Tax, Sol
Evolution After Darwin. Volume I: The Evolution of Life. Volume II: The Evolution of Man. Volume III: Issues in Evolution. The University of Chicago, Centennial Discussions, 1960.

Teilhard de Chardin, Pierre
The Future of Man. Harper & Row, New York 1964.

Thompson, D'Arcy
Of Growth and Form. University Press, Cambridge 1945.

Thoreau, Henry
Walden and other Writings. The Modern Library, New York 1937.

Toynbee, Arnold J., ed.
Greek Historical Thought from Homer to the Age of Heraclitus. New American Library, New York 1964.

Van der Velde, Henry
Geschichte meines Lebens. Piper, 1962.

Von Simson, Otto
The Gothic Cathedral. Bollingen Series, Second Edition, 1962.

Waley, Arthur
Yuan Mei. Eighteenth Century Chinese Poet. George Allen and Unwin Ltd., London 1956.

Weiss, Paul
The World of Art. Southern Illinois University Press, 1961.

Weizsäcker, C. F. v.
The Relevance of Science, Creation and Cosmology. Collins, London 1964.
The History of Nature. The University of Chicago Press, 1949.
Die Tragweite der Wissenschaft, Band 1. S. Hirzel Verlag, Stuttgart 1966.
Zum Weltbild der Physik. S. Hirzel Verlag, Stuttgart 1963.
The World View of Physics. University of Chicago Press (1949), 1952.

Werkbund
Jahrbuch 1913: Die Kunst in Industrie und Handel.
Jahrbuch 1914: Der Verkehr.

Weyl, Hermann
Symmetrie. Princeton University Press, 1952.

Whitehead, Alfred North
Dialogues of Alfred North as recorded by Lucien Price. Little Brown, Boston 1954
Adventures of Ideas. Macmillan, New York 1947.
Science and the Modern World. The New American Library, New York 1948.

Whyte, Lancelot Law
Aspects of Form, A Symposium on Form in Nature and Art. Pellegrini & Cudahy, New York 1951.

Ziegler, Leopold
Florentinische Introduktion. Felix Meiner Verlag, Leipzig 1912.
Zwischen Mensch und Wirtschaft. Otto Reichl Verlag, 1927.

German Pavilion, Barcelona 1928–1929

The German pavilion at the International Exhibition in Barcelona is held to be one of the masterpieces of the 20th century. To mark Mies' 100th birthday this building with its patios was reconstructed on its original site and opened to the public.

Mies quoted a dictum of St. Augustine: "Beauty is the splendour of truth."

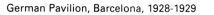

German Pavilion, Barcelona, 1928-1929

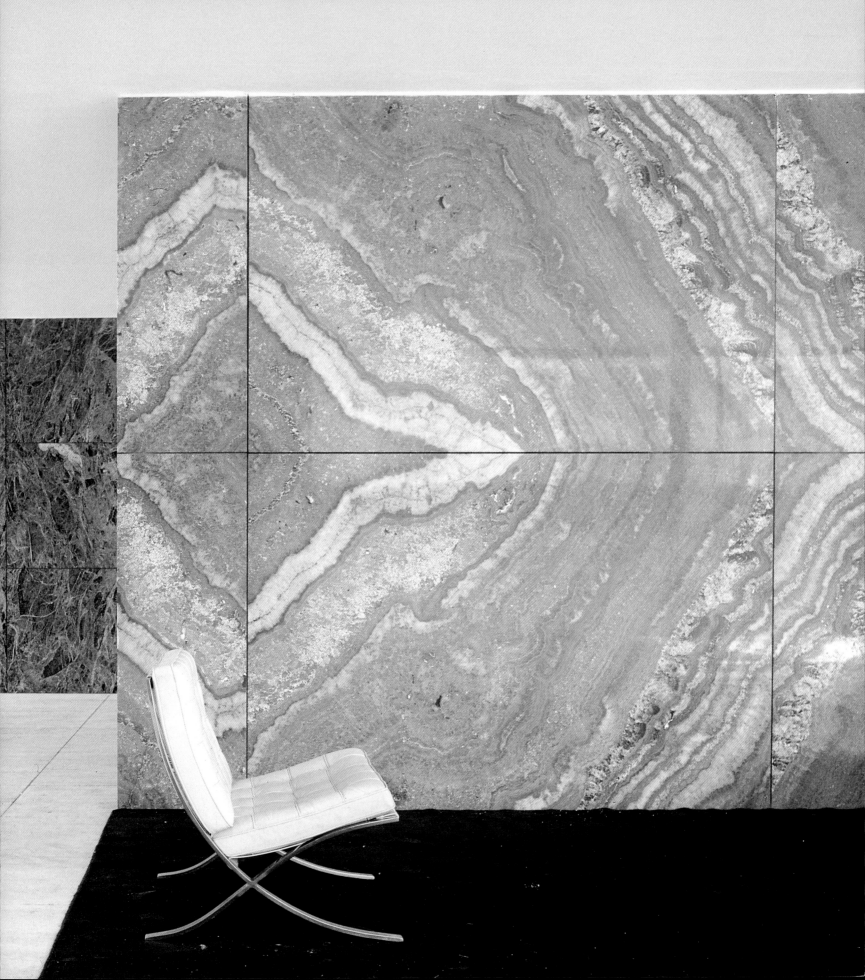

Farnsworth House at Plano, Illinois, 1945–1950

The one-room week-end house on the Fox River has been restored to its previous condition. The interior was furnished with Mies classics – the Tugendhat and Brno chairs. Regarding this building,

Mies once said: "I feel that the Farnsworth House has never been properly understood. I was in this house myself from morning till evening. I had never known till then what splendid colours nature can display. The interior must therefore be kept neutral in tone because there are all the colours outside. These colours are continually changing throughout, and I should like to say that it is simply marvellous."

860–880 Lake Shore Drive Apartments, 1948–1951
and 900 Lake Shore Drive Apartments, 1953–1956

"High, higher, highest" is the motto in Chicago.
The first photographs of these buildings dating
from 1951 are to be found in the main section
(pp.128). This is a photo taken in 1983 with the
John Hancock Center (1210 ft.) by Skidmore,
Owings & Merrill.

Mies said: "When you plan, don't think just of the
hammer. Take your trumpet. Building needs
resounding ideas." And the Chicago city-planner
Daniel Burnham said: "Don't make small plans!
They haven't got the magic it needs to make the
blood pulse in the veins. Make big plans. In your
work set your sights as high as possible. Others
are going to scale it down anyway."

236

Federal Center in Chicago, 1959–1973

By massing the design in two superblocks of 30 and 45 storeys, it was possible to achieve a spacious downtown area with detached buildings in the densely built-up business centre of the "Loop". The post office is a flat-roofed building with a column-free interior measuring 60 × 60 metres and glazed on all sides, set back from the street so that a free space, a "plaza", is created. Mies, however, did not avail himself of this domain, and the large open spaces evoke a friendly impression welcoming to citizens. It was not until 1974 that Alexander Calder's red steel structure "Flamingo" was set up in the square in front of the black high-rise buildings and the post office and integrated as a major sculpture.

"I don't want to be interesting, I want to be good" is perhaps Mies' most important statement.

238

ALBUQUERQUE ACADEMY
LIBRARY
6400 Wyoming Blvd. N.E.
Albuquerque, N.M. 87109